One of the Lost Returns

One of the Lost Returns

A Journey Back to Christ

Bryan Paul Gomes

XULON PRESS

Xulon Press
2301 Lucien Way #415
Maitland, FL 32751
407.339.4217
www.xulonpress.com

Paperback ISBN-13: 978-1-6628-3955-9
Ebook ISBN-13: 978-1-6628-4237-5

WRITTEN BY:
BRYAN GOMES

INSPIRED BY:
THE HOLY SPIRIT

BIRTHDATE
OCTOBER 9, 1974

BORN AGAIN
JULY 7, 2021

A NEW FAMILY IN CHRIST:

A PASSING AWAY OF THE OLD DYSFUNCTIONAL FAMILY OF THE WORLD:

Everything I write is from the Spirit of Christ in me for reproof and teaching of the Holy Spirit (not me but Him) and received by the Spirit in those who seek to know our Lord and Savior Jesus Christ deeper and closer than you ever have before. I offer nothing of myself only what you the reader receives from the Holy Spirit

Christ Jesus is my brother and God is my Father we are that close in Spirit I do not say these things for any self-gratification only that others will see my relationship with the Father and the Son as a Family together in Love and Grace with a Peace that is not known or found anywhere else in the world but only in a personal intimate relationship with Jesus Christ and our Heavenly Father.

ARE YOU READY TO BE CHANGED FOR ETERNITY?

CONTENTS

THE SOLDIERS DECREE TO CHRIST IN THE ARMY OF THE FATHER OF ALL CREATION

NO CHILD OF GOD LEFT BEHIND.

(This requires an active faith in the physical world and in the battlefield of the mind)

I DO NOT SWEAR BUT SAY YES WITH MY HEART TO MY FATHER WHO HAS CREATED ME IN HIS IMAGE BY THE SPIRIT OF CHRIST JESUS THAT I WILL KEEP MY TEMPLE (my mind) PURE AND CLEAN IN HIS RIGHTEOUSNESS.

I WILL PUT ONLY GOD FIRST AND SPEAK ONLY OF THE TEACHINGS OF THE WORD OF

CHRIST IN EVERY ASPECT OF MY LIFE WHICH WAS GIVEN TO ME BY YOU MY FATHER

RECEIVED THROUGH THE HOLY SPIRIT AND IN ALL MY ACTIONS SO THAT MY TREE

(My body) WILL ONLY BEAR FRUIT WHICH GIVES LOVE, PATIENCE, KINDNESS, GOODNESS

AND MERCY TO ALL WHO SEEK TO

EAT FROM IT. AND ONLY UTTER WORDS FROM MY LIPS OF THE EVERLASTING WATER OF TRUTH.

IF EVER I SHOULD FALTER FROM ANY OF THEE ABOVE, I WILL SURRENDER MYSELF

BACK TO THE LORD MY GOD FOR REPROACH AND RE-TEACHING AS THIS IS MY ONLY MISSION OF RIGHTEOUSNESS, WORTHINESS AND GLORY TO THE ONE AND ONLY FATHER OF ALL CREATION IN THIS EARTH AND OF ALL THE HEAVENS.

This is the last will and testament of my old life of selfishness and disobedience and by this I claim to live now a Crucified life in service and sacrifice of all who I am and receive all of Christ in my place.

I now come to you humbled and broken as a bond-servant underneath all those who I speak to through the gift of Christ Jesus and the teaching of Your Word received in me and to cleanse me of my inequities and to not do YOUR work but that YOUR WILL be done through me.

Signed: ***Bryan Paul Gomes***

MY BEGINNING

A BEGINNING IN CHRIST

A Memoir: My life back to Christ by Bryan Paul Gomes

Born in Portland Oregon

1974

Lived in Duluth Minnesota when I was two and back to Portland

Grew up in the house we are now residing in, in southeast Portland Oregon) grew up playing sports played soccer as a kid for 13 years then basketball and learned how to golf when I was incredibly young.

Worked for the Portland trailblazers as a team attendant for visiting teams. I worked directly with all the old players personally (Barkley Jordan Magic Drexler Isaiah etc. etc.)

Never had idols as I worked for many famous people growing up and to me, they are just people.

Went to public school then a private school and found out it was not credited by the state, so I got my Ged.

And printed a regular diploma to join the army for the bonus money in 1992

Met my wife Pam in 1995 at a dance club called quest we dated for a few months and then by surprise,

She was pregnant 3 months later (my son was born high functioning autistic and was awfully hard on us emotionally)

(He is now fully committed to God)

My wife and I got Married in 1996

(25 years married this last July 8th, 2021)

We then moved to Illesheim Germany as I was stationed with the 2-6 air calvary 11th aviation regiment (Apache Helicopters) from 1997 to 2000

Our daughter was born in Germany in 1999 (in Europe the father delivers the baby this was the most beautiful and amazing experience to do.

E.T.S. from active duty and 6 months after returning to Portland I enlisted with the 162nd infantry battalion as a mechanic from 2000 to 2006.

Deployed 1 week after Hurricane Katrina hit New Orleans (we were based in the lower ninth ward clearing houses and transporting stuff and not so good stuff) Got out after the tour was not right in the head after that deployment lost lots of buddies during my years in service.

In 2010 I went to school to become a tattoo artist

(I was taught by the son of Lew Lewis who collaborated with sailor Jerry and Ed hardy in the 50s) Got licensed and been tattooing ever since (not much anymore) (ask and I will show you some work privately)

got into the club scene lots and lots of self-medicating with ecstasy and Cocaine on weekends.

Got in trouble for a conspiracy ecstasy deal and got a class A felony for it (worst kind)

Took a dip in depression P.T.S.D. and the likes from the military got back into the cocaine, family life was trash because of my inequities.

Out of the blue during the covid thing we started the Patriot Conspiracy stuff I stopped the drug use and scripture was the focus that started it all for me.

And here is where I started my path back home to our Father.

A new thing created in me from the start comes alive. Started with a look at a dusty Bible at the beginning of a fake pandemic that God used to take away all that was between Him and my selfish ambitions. After a year and a half of following clues and going to scripture and back to all the things in the world to find answers to all the things I did not understand on my own, But I was rapidly starting to find peace in the scriptures and still struggled to know why. Why all this and why now?

Why am I one foot in and one foot out and confused.

Fast forward to July 9th ,2021. When God called my spirit from the heavens and flipped my confusion to clarity like nothing the world has ever known I was dropped to my knees in the kitchen in the morning and was taken from myself.

Here is that story...

My true spiritual understanding of me that exists in Christ Jesus

Started July 9th, 2020

And 2 days prior on July 7th, 2020, this happened....

Dad asked me in a loud earth-shattering voice from my soul

Was given this scripture in Spirit

And I heard the voice of the Lord saying, "Whom shall I send, and who will go for us?" Then I said, "Here I am! Send me."

And my response to Him: I said SEND ME

I was Commissioned now to live a life of re-teaching each person I come in contact with the Gospel of Christ, God's word that is in them so that they may find their way back to the Father Isaiah 6:8 is my Commission to God.

This path back to Him for some is a brick by brick taking down all the walls we have built ourselves and without His instruction it falls as a house on the sand.

My closet had to come clean and clean by my standards was not what He wanted, it was a 3am every day for 3 ½ months on my knees in a puddle of tears showing me all of my iniquities and times I have hurt others and Him and all of my not so public thoughts and feelings some I never even knew I had. This was absolutely the most terrifying heart wrenching, humiliating thing ever and from time to time there were some amazing gems of memories I had buried under all the filth in my life. He knew He could not do this brick by brick with me as I would backslide as I had many times before, so He bulldozed the filthy castle I built for myself and let me wallow in the sadness I created all with loving arms wrapped around me to comfort me in the process.

I am now the true man in the mirror that He sees

And I love His view of the me he made me

I Love you Father, thank you for calling me home to you

This from Apostle Paul: (also my middle name)

I myself am satisfied about you, my brothers, that you yourselves are full of goodness, filled with all knowledge and able to instruct one another. But on some points, I have written to you very boldly by way of reminder, because of the grace given me by God to be a minister of Christ

Jesus to the Gentiles in the priestly service of the gospel of God, so that the offering of the Gentiles may be acceptable, sanctified by the Holy Spirit. In Christ Jesus, then, I have reason to be proud of my work for God. For I will not venture to speak of anything except what Christ has accomplished through me to bring the Gentiles to obedience–by word and deed, by the power of signs and wonders, by the power of the Spirit of God–so that from Jerusalem and all the way around to Illyricum I have fulfilled the ministry of the gospel of Christ; and thus I make it my ambition to preach the gospel, not where Christ has already been named, lest I build on someone else's foundation, but as it is written, "Those who have never been told of him will see, and those who have never heard will .

The spirit of God the creator of heaven and earth and all of creation who is Christ Jesus within each of us since resurrection Has given us the gift of eternal life

God has already won the battle

The scriptures will play out in the spirit as the physical battle of the world will be all of God's prophecies fulfilled.

MY HEART'S PRAYER:

I COME TO YOU

MY LORD AND SAVIOR

THIS I BRING TO YOU EVERY MORNING AND EVERY WAKING MOMENT. I COME TO YOU IN HUMILITY AND BROKENNESS ...O LORD I SURRENDER MY EVERY FEELING, MY EVERY THOUGHT, MY EVERY ACTION MY EVERY WORD SPOKEN, I SURRENDER IT ALL TO YOU O LORD. FOR WITHOUT YOU I AM NOTHING, AND I OWE EVERYTHING I HAVE TO YOU LORD BE MY FOUNDATION, BE MY PILLOW, BE MY SHIELD, BE MY ROCK, BE MY WATER, BE MY BREATH, BE EVERYTHING I AM. FOR I AM NOTHING WITHOUT YOU. LET NOTHING COME FROM MY MOUTH OR MY HEART THAT IS NOT OF YOU. I SURRENDER COMPLETELY AND WHOLLY TO YOU POWER AND MERCY AND LOVING GRACE, MAKE ME YOUR TOOL AND LET YOUR WILL BE DONE THROUGH ME LORD LET YOUR LIGHT SHINE THROUGH EVERY PART OF MY BEING SO THAT ALL I TOUCH ALL I FEEL ALL I THINK ALL I SAY, BE OF YOUR WISDOM TRUTH AND PRAISE

LORD
I
SURRENDER

YOU CAN'T FIX IT ALONE:

(When we stop thinking about all the things we need to fix in our own lives and trying to figure out how to solve others' problems, as if we even know where to start, nor do we have any solutions for matters pertaining to the heart of anyone's suffering.)

who comforts us in all our affliction so that we will be able to comfort those who are in any affliction with the comfort with which we ourselves are comforted by God. For just as the sufferings of Christ are ours in abundance, so also our comfort is abundant through Christ.
2 Corinthians 1:4

(When you have come to the end of your rope and have exhausted all efforts and have no more strategies to try, You are not defeated, No You are at the beginning of a place that you may not recognize, it is in a weird way comforting and frightening at the same time. This is the place deep inside you where **devastation** turns into **salvation.)**

Blessed be the God and Father of our Lord Jesus Christ, the Father of mercies and God of all comfort,
2 Corinthians 1:3 NASB

Search me, O God, and know my heart; Try me and know my anxious thoughts; And see if there be any hurtful way in me And lead me in the everlasting way.
Psalms 139:23

(See this broken place you have come to in your life, it was going to happen sooner or later and in a weird way in the back of your mind you knew it would come, most don't admit it to themselves or recognize this is exactly where God wants them to be to receive His Grace and Mercy for their suffering, they have caused themselves by ignoring Him and doing everything their own way like a spoiled child, or a self-righteous man. This place of emptiness you are in is where the Holy Spirit of God is going to speak to you From within that broken place if you choose to listen with a open heart.)
(Have you ever had that deep, deep, chest grabbing sadness and feeling like your whole body could just fall apart and crumble into pieces?) There is someone I know very, very well, closer than a brother to me He is kind of a Big Big deal to the entire world, But so many don't realize this ot they ignore the good news till they get to this point where you might be at (broken and helpless, ready to give up and call it quits.) That deep crushing pain and sadness that you have in places you don't have words to explain. This guy My Friend, My Brother, My Comforter, My Peace, My Joy, My Hope, My Faith, My Understanding,
My Wisdom, My Everything. He can take that from you and fill you with so much Peace and Love that it feels like you will explode into party confetti of unimaginable measures. His name, is the name above all names, Prince of Peace, Mighty Lord, Conquer of all Death, Savior, King of Kings, Lord of Lords.)

In the same way the Spirit also helps our weakness; for we do not know how to pray as we should, but the Spirit Himself intercedes for us with groanings too deep for words; and He who

searches the hearts knows what the mind of the Spirit is, because He intercedes for the saints according to the will of God.
Romans 8:26

(This guy I know they call Him Jesus and He is the Christ, the Son of The Living God Our Father of all creation of the Heavens and Earth. I'm wanting to introduce Him to you if you have not met Him yet
And more than anything in my own life which belongs to Him now, I want you to know Jesus as close as I have come to know Him, He wants more than anything to walk and talk and be with you all day every day in every thought you think, every joyous victory, every loss, every gain, every fear and I mean even the fear of death itself He will take from you and replace it with a Peace that cannot be comprehended in any fashion.)

(I leave you this invitation spoken by my Friend, Brother and Savior of my life Jesus Christ.

Once you hear Him and open the door don't look back, your entire existence of what you thought you were and what will be revealed to you by the Holy Spirit will take your breath out of your chest and replace it with a wonder that cannot be Spoken into words.)

Dear Child of mine,
Behold, I stand at the door and knock; if anyone hears My voice and opens the door, I will come into him and will dine with him, and he with Me. He who overcomes, I will grant to him to sit down with Me on My throne, as I also overcame and sat down with My Father on His throne.
Revelation 3:20

Welcome Home,
Where You Belong
In His Arms
Family Once Again.

THE COMMISION:

To begin this, I want the reader of these words to see my writing as a window to God as I am of no greater understanding of God's Word by myself than any other man as it is the Wisdom of the Holy Spirit that guides all aspects of my life and so it is He who speaks through me. My prayer is that you hear God's Words, and a stirring of your soul brings you to Him and the reader will forget me and cling to God only.

Just as in the days of the prophet Isaiah God Speaks and we receive Wisdom from the Holy Spirit not our flesh do we receive but our Spiritual body because we are born a new creation in Christ Jesus.

And this is the only way one can understand what is spoken in scripture. It is not our own interpretation of what we read but we receive it in our heart where only God knows.

Isaiah 6:8
Then I heard the voice of the Lord, saying, "Whom shall I send, and who will go for Us?" Then I said, "Here am I. Send me!"

(Isaiah heard God speak and answered the Question that was asked knowing the eternal importance of what was at hand for all who would hear the call of the Lord and turn from a life of ignorance and disobedience to God and be healed.)

Isaiah 6:9
He said, "Go, and tell these people: 'Keep on listening, but do not perceive; Keep on looking, but do not understand.' Render the hearts of these people insensitive, their ears dull, and their eyes dim, otherwise they might see with their eyes, hear with their ears, understand with their hearts, and return and be healed."

Isaiah receives instruction (Commission)directly from God to Tell all who have eyes but are blind and who have ears but are deaf (They are not looking to God or listening to God, but instead listening and looking for truth in everything else.)

(He is told to render the hearts of these people who are deaf and blind to God insensitive)

Matthew 13:15 NASB
Jesus says for the heart of these people has become dull, with their ears they scarcely hear,
And they have closed their eyes, otherwise they would see with their eyes, Hear with their ears,
And understand with their heart and return, And I would heal them.'

Isaiah 6:11

Then I said, "Lord, how long?" And He answered, "Until cities are devastated and without inhabitant, Houses are without people and the land is utterly desolate,

(How long am I to do this? Isaiah asks the Lord. God wants all things broken and battered and laid waste so that all will come to hear His voice and seek Him, and He will take everything away until we put Him 1st even before our most cherished possessions.)

Isaiah 6:12
The Lord has removed men far away, And the forsaken places are many in the midst of the land.

(Deuteronomy 28:64
Moreover, the Lord will scatter you among all peoples, from one end of the earth to the other end of the earth; and there you shall serve other gods, wood and stone, which you or your fathers have not known.)(this is all people all over the world God is talking about look around you with politics, leaders ,pastors,, men of good stature, these are the people that everyone is looking for answers of truth from and therefore are blind and deaf to God's Words.)

Isaiah 6:13a
Yet there will be a tenth portion in it, and it will again be subject to burning,

(Job 14:7)
"For there is hope for a tree, when it is cut down, that it will sprout again, And its shoots will not fail.)

(This is the Everlasting Life we receive when we die to self and are reborn in Christ.)

Isaiah 6:13b
Like a terebinth or an oak Whose stump remains when it is felled. The holy seed is its stump."

When we accept Christ and believe and walk by Faith not by sight, for it is what is seen is of the world, God created that which is not seen but revealed to us by the Holy Spirit who is all Wisdom of God.

When we seek God first and always in all things and lean not on our own understanding but receive teaching and instruction from Christ through the Holy Spirit.

For Christ Jesus is the Holy Seed of Life given to us by God that we will be saved from all that will come to destruction and lay waste as it is God's Will and God's Word that will be fulfilled not ours.

"We change nothing, we are called to be fishers of men, not reporters of world news."

I have taken Commission as Isaiah did. Then not I but Christ in me as I have no need for any admiration and only speak that all may hear with the Holy Spirit and receive God's Words not mine.

WHO I'VE BECOME:

I cannot apologize for the sorrows I see in others that I feel for they are not of my own understanding but put upon my heart by the Holy Spirit and any conviction that is felt by my words, may it be harsh sounding at times it is not from my lips that these words are uttered but from Christ as He has shown me what it truly means to bear one's own cross not in the sense of the physical world but one of a deeper pain and sorrow that only He knows and is revealing to me as I seek only to live as He did in all ways. Not that I am any different than the next man for I seek only to live by His example, and He is my counsel and my Pride and having put away all things of me to live as His Will be done not mine.

HEAVENLY VISION AND THE VOICE OF WISDOM:

(Not by anything we have done or can do but by the loving Grace of our Father and through His Son Jesus Christ we have received the Holy Spirit which and been redeemed from death to be born again and have an eternal life in Christ Jesus.)

He then answered, "Whether He is a sinner, I do not know; one thing I do know, that though I was blind, now I see."
John 9:25 NASB

Come and hear, all who fear God, And I will tell of what He has done for my soul.
Psalms 66:16 NASB

But the free gift is not like the transgression. For if by the transgression of the one the many died, much more did the grace of God and the gift by the grace of the one Man, Jesus Christ, abound to the many. The gift is not like that which came through the one who sinned; for on the one hand the judgment arose from one transgression resulting in condemnation, but on the other hand the free gift arose from many transgressions resulting in justification. For if by the transgression of the one, death reigned through the one, much more those who receive the abundance of grace and of the gift of righteousness will reign in life through the One, Jesus Christ.
Romans 5:15

CRUCIFIED LIFE:

This will create a whirlwind of emotions and maybe Casting of Judgment towards me by those that know me and cause some to not understand me and be very confused and I am 100% ok with that as I am committed to fully knowing my Savior so intimately so much so that I

know I will feel very lonely at times but knowing that with Him I am never alone.

For it is Him that I seek to please and for Him alone do I want to live. Having a deep conversation with my Savior this morning over coffee and a bagel.

I know without question that the political and new Government movement of the United States and current theology of united one religion in the majority of the church's movement offering peace and wealth and freedom from the evils of the world is a preparing for the coming of the Antichrist

(There have been many but there is one that will offer all things of the world that will be pleasing to all men great and small)

This is a great deception as Christ Jesus offers us not things that are seen but things that are not seen by the world.

We are to seek Him First and love Him above all else even more so than our own life or the ones we love Just as Abram brought Isaac his 1st love and only son to God when asked we are to live a life Christ First to be Glorified by our Father as it is not by our own works that the Fathers will be done but by the Spirit of Christ who dwells in us ,should we seek Him and surrender ourselves to His Glory and Worship Him in all we are.

Let us not be just hearers of the Word but be doers in all we do as to bring glory to our Father.

Let us not be pulled away from His glory with promises of great things.

Or be tempted by the feelings of freedom from those that speak not of the freedom in Christ Jesus.

Or be tricked into the thoughts that give us false hope in things that will lead us to destruction.

For how we can alone sail this vessel to a destination not known to us, just as a map and compass,

A Captain and one who knows the course on the map are needed,

So do we need Christ Jesus, God's Word, and the guidance of the Holy spirit to set sail and return to our Heavenly Father who So patiently awaits our return to Him.

Though the Storms may come His love for us will endure all things and we will weather all of them with His peace that surpasses all understanding.

We are going to get wet, and it will be hard to see at times with the wind and rain, wipe your brow, stand at the bow, and know that the one that is at the wheel knows the direction and the captain of your vessel is the King of Kings and Lord of Lords.

His Love abounds and because of Him we will not grow weary or faint

But will stand fast in various trials knowing that His goodness and Grace are all that we need.

One must understand that not all scripture will be understood by all people "he who has an ear let him hear what the Spirit is saying"

This requires one to be living a full life devoted solely to Christ as in being dead to the ways of the world and the thoughts and understandings of self but to die of self and to live for Christ. Even what I am saying may be misinterpreted by those who have not died in themselves and been born a new creation in Christ Jesus.

TO LIVE IS CHRIST TO DIE IS GAIN

(If we die to self, we gain life in Christ Jesus)

For we should choose to live only then will one truly understand that our Father is a personal Father who wants a very personal intimate relationship with each one of us.

Just as you stand outside and see with your eye's things of this world

You should seek to see your Father the same way and this is only done through Christ.

One cannot use scripture to protect themselves from a life that they live that is not a life of Christ

.For instance, using psalms 23 when you are at the bar every weekend and living a life not pleasing to Christ does not work. This is where He says I do not know you.

Galatians 2:20
"I am Crucified with Christ; nevertheless, I live; yet not I, but Christ liveth in me; And the life which I now live in the flesh I live by the faith of the Son of God, who loved me, and gave Himself for me."

(James 4:6-10 NASB)
But He gives a greater grace. Therefore, it says, "God is opposed to the proud, but gives grace to the humble." Submit therefore to God. Resist the devil and he will flee from you. Draw near to God and He will draw near to you. Cleanse your hands, you sinners; and purify your hearts, you double-minded. Be miserable and mourn and weep; let your laughter be turned into mourning and your joy to gloom. Humble yourselves in the presence of the Lord, and He will exalt you.

PATIENTS:

AS NEWBORN IN CHRIST:

Therefore, putting aside all malice, all deceit, hypocrisy, envy, and all slander, like newborn babies, long for the pure milk of the word, so that by it you may grow in respect to salvation, if you have tasted the kindness of the Lord.
1 Peter 2:1-2

(What in your daily life are you taking part in just as the rest of the world does? Who do you talk bad about just to follow the ones you fit in with? What are those in Christ called to be? We have seen the kindness of the Lord and we must need and want His teaching just as an infant need and wants their mothers nourishment.)

AS LIVING STONES:

And coming to Him as to a living stone which has been rejected by men but is choice and precious in the sight of God, you also, as living stones, are being built up as a spiritual house for a holy priesthood, to offer up spiritual sacrifices acceptable to God through Jesus Christ. For this is contained in Scripture: "Behold, I lay in Zion a choice stone, a precious corner stone, And he who believes in Him will not be disappointed." This precious value, then, is for you who believe; but for those who disbelieve, "The stone which the builders rejected, This became the very corner stone," and, "A stone of stumbling and a rock of offense;" for they stumble because they are disobedient to the word, and to this doom they were also appointed. But you are a chosen race, a royal priesthood, a holy nation, a people for God's own possession, so that you may proclaim the excellencies of Him who has called you out of darkness into His marvelous light; for you once were not a people, but now you are the people of God; you had not received mercy, but now you have received mercy. Beloved, I urge you as aliens and strangers to abstain from fleshly lusts which wage war against the soul. Keep your behavior excellent among the Gentiles, so that in the thing in which they slander you as evildoers, they may because of your good deeds, as they observe them, glorify God in the day of visitation.
1 Peter 2:3-12

(Those in Christ are precious to God and not like the rest.
Be not conformed to things as the world is conformed to things, we must be found blameless in our Fathers eyes, and this means the world and those that have not found Christ will be attracted to the fruit that the Spirit produces through our works by Faith in Christ Jesus.)

HONOR AUTHORITY:

Submit yourselves for the Lord's sake to every human institution, whether to a king as the one in authority, or to governors as sent by him for the punishment of evildoers and the praise of those who do right. For such is the will of God that by doing right you may silence the ignorance of foolish men. Act as free men, and do not use your freedom as a covering for evil but use it as bondslaves of God. Honor all people, love the brotherhood, fear God, honor the king. Servants, be submissive to your masters with all respect, not only to those who are good and gentle, but also to those who are unreasonable. For this finds favor, if for the sake of conscience toward God a person bears up under sorrows when suffering unjustly. For what credit is there if, when you sin and are harshly treated, you endure it with patience? But if when you do what is right and suffer for it you patiently endure it, this finds favor with God.
1 Peter 2:13

(This one is going to strike a chord with most of you. We are called to 1) Love the Lord your God with all your Heart, Soul, Mind, Body and Strength 2) Love your neighbor as yourself. Yes, that means you cannot distinguish which person you like or dislike, this includes your co-workers, family members, Politicians, Judges, Presidents, Movie Stars, Musicians etc. etc.
For the world cries and whines and complains when they are treated badly even when they are doing wrong just the same when they are doing what they think is right.

We are called to patiently endure hardships from those we agree with and even those we do not agree with, without grumbling or complaining. This is pleasing to our Father.)

CHRIST IS OUR EXAMPLE:

For you have been called for this purpose, since Christ also suffered for you, leaving you an example for you to follow in His steps, who committed no sin, nor was any deceit found in His mouth; and while being reviled, He did not revile in return; while suffering, He uttered no threats, but kept entrusting Himself to Him who judges righteously; and He Himself bore our sins in His body on the cross, so that we might die to sin and live to righteousness; for by His wounds you were healed. For you were continually straying like sheep, but now you have returned to the Shepherd and Guardian of your souls.
1 Peter 2:21

(To be born again means to be as Christ is and to live as He taught us. Today as in everyday if our Lord and Savior returned at this moment would He be pleased with what you are thinking about?
What are you watching?
What are you talking about?
Are you complaining about things just as your friends are?
Are you being complicit in conversation at your church with followers who are doing these things?
These are the tough growing pains of a crucified life in Christ we must live with and overcome just as Christ died for us, we must live according to Him and put the old self to death by continuing to seek Him in all ways for all teaching so that we may be found pleasing to Him when He comes for us.)

HUMILITY:

God wants all His children to live a humble life and show humility to everyone.

Humility is not only a mindset it is an attitude that comes from the heart.

True humility cannot be seen on the outside; it can only be felt directly from the heart.

When you are humble, you are not prideful, selfish, or arrogant. Humility is not something you gain overnight; humility is revealed increasingly as you grow in grace, wisdom, and understanding.

God not only causes you to be humble, but He also expects you to be humble.

God tells us in (2 Chronicles 7:14:) "Then if my people who are called by my name will humble themselves and pray and seek my face and turn from their wicked ways, I will hear from heaven and will forgive their sins and restore their land."

Biblically speaking, humility is the opposite of pride, arrogance, and self-importance.

God will oppose those who are arrogant, proud, and self-centered, but He has promised to give grace to those who are humble based on the true motives of their heart.

(James 4:13-17 NASB)
Come now, you who say, "Today or tomorrow we will go to such and such a city and spend a year there and engage in business and make a profit.

(For God's Will is our Destination not our desires and wants and when we choose to let Him Guide our every aspect of life there is no greater path than this.)

" Yet you do not know what your life will be like tomorrow. You are just a vapor that appears for a little while and then vanishes away. Instead, you ought to say, "If the Lord wills, we will live and also do this or that." But as it is, you boast in your arrogance; all such boasting is evil. Therefore, to one who knows the right thing to do and does not do it, to him it is sin.

(The most cliche saying ever used but still to this day has the most important bit of Wisdom is this...LET GO...LET GOD!) try it and you will never take another path again this is God's Promise of Mercy and Grace.)

THE GREAT DECEPTION:

I do not write this to bring fear no but to warn all who hear these words and take them to the Holy spirit in prayer as to discern what comes from my words not I but Christ who is within me through the Holy Spirit.

He has put forth his hands against those who were at peace with him; He has violated his covenant. His speech was smoother than butter, but his heart was warm; His words were softer than oil, yet they were drawn swords.
Psalms 55:20-21

(This calls for wisdom of the Holy Spirit) hear what the Spirit speaks to you as you will receive from Him not by these words.

And Jesus answered and said to them, "See to it that no one misleads you. For many will come in My name, saying, 'I am the Christ,' and will mislead many. You will be hearing of wars and rumors of wars. See that you are not frightened, for those things must take place, but that is not yet the end. For nation will rise against nation, and kingdom against kingdom, and in various places there will be famines and earthquakes. But all these things are merely the beginning of birth pangs. "Then they will deliver you to tribulation, and will kill you, and you will be hated by all nations because of My name. At that time many will fall away and will betray one another and hate one another. Many false prophets will arise and will mislead many. Because lawlessness

is increased, most people's love will grow cold. But the one who endures to the end, he will be saved. This gospel of the kingdom shall be preached in the whole world as a testimony to all the nations, and then the end will come.
Matthew 24:4-14 NASB

Then read
DANIEL 11 AND 12

nesara and gesara are all part of the beast system.
(Quantum computers)
All of it is Alchemy just as all the architecture from the days of antiquitech/tartaria was all built by god's that were cast out of heaven. Extension of Babylonian Empire.

The saviors of the world that are (being shown) and all this talk of the truth in the world is all the same thing as the evil

The evil and the globalist (1st beast) satanic ones will be brought to light and crushed by the new government and military (image of the beast)
Then everyone will praise the ones who brought freedom to the world
But they signed the deal with the dragon serpent Satan

But they do not have the truth only
That they are the saviors of the evil
All of this is to set up the "abomination of desolation"
(Dark to light)

Bringing out the evil to appear like the Savior of humankind.

(Daniel 12:8-11)
As for me, I heard but could not understand; so, I said, "My Lord, what will be the outcome of these events?" He said, "Go your

way, Daniel, for these words are concealed and sealed up until the end time. Many will be purged, purified, and refined, but the wicked will act wickedly; and none of the wicked will understand, but those who have insight will understand. From the time that the regular sacrifice is abolished, and the abomination of desolation is set up, there will be 1,290 days.)

3.5 years of cleaning the swamp and getting rid of evil.

Then comes false freedom offered by the 2nd beast. Financial freedom and saved from the evils of 1st beast (the US signed the Abraham accords which was with the cursed Israel.

Daniel 12:12 How blessed is he who keeps waiting and attains to the 1,335 days!
1290-1335 = 45 days

45 days of peace and prosperity
Just as in the days of Noah
All will be drinking and being merry with wealth and freedom as it is written.

This requires wisdom from the Holy Spirit
But seek first His kingdom and His righteousness, and all these things will be added to you. Matthew 6:33

Do not be wise as the world is for it is not the kingdom of God and much destruction will come to those who do not make Christ Jesus their Lord and savior.

And then from within the image of the beast comes a great one that all will adore and admire. This is the Antichrist, and he will rule with an iron scepter, and all will worship him, and he will offer peace and prosperity and eternal life to all who worship him and to receive the mark.

This is the great Deception Not the great Awakening.
JESUS CHRIST IS THE ONLY SAVIOR

THE WAY
THE TRUTH
AND THE LIFE

NO ONE COMES TO THE FATHER BUT BY ME SAYS THE LORD.

Cast your burden upon the Lord and He will sustain you; He will never allow the righteous to be shaken. But You, O God, will bring them down to the pit of destruction; Men of bloodshed and deceit will not live out half their days. But I will trust in You. Psalms 55:22-23

Rejoice in the Lord always; again, I will say, rejoice! Let your gentle spirit be known to all men. The Lord is nearby. Be anxious for nothing, but in everything by prayer and supplication with thanksgiving let your requests be made known to God. Philippians 4:4-6 NASB

Do not fall down brothers and sisters and say, I am weak, or I am too tired and can't go on for this is the serpent's tricks to boast in our weakness for it is not us but Christ who has defeated death.

And He is in us through the grace of our Father that we remain to fight the good fight not to draw the sword ourselves but to love our God and stand in the midst of evil even up to death as we know that those that come to kill all who love Him and put Him First above all things. Will fall at our feet because Great vengeance will come to those who have come against His Glory and deceived His Children

But Christ who is in you gives you strength when you are weak

And He has said to me, "My grace is sufficient for you, for power is perfected in weakness." Most gladly, therefore, I will rather boast about my weaknesses, so that the power of Christ may dwell in me. Therefore, I am well content with weaknesses, with insults, with distresses, with persecutions, with difficulties, for Christ's sake; for when I am weak, then I am strong. 2 Corinthians 12:9-10

Brothers and sisters be not concerned with all the comings and goings of the world and the news

For we know that all things come and go as spoken by the prophets of old and yet given to us in such clarity for these days they knew not of by the truth of the Holy Spirit.

And in turn do not let the truth of the world which we know to be folly come from your lips as it will only deceive and confuse those you speak to.
Let us only speak of what Is from the Holy Spirit, truth through the scriptures and as it is revealed to us in prayer and quiet time with our Lord and Savior.

For it is better to bite off your tongue than to speak a word that will cause one of God's children to stumble.

It is not I who know these things nor my wisdom, of which I have none.
But it is by the truth of Christ given to me by The Holy Spirit who is the Word of God made whole in me.

It is not truth the world cannot offer what the world does not understand

The devil is a liar, and he rules this world

Do not be conformed to the world but be transformed by the renewing of your mind that you may seek the truth only found in Christ Jesus through the gift of God the Holy Spirit who is the Word of God spoken to you by God Himself.

It is not I that know or have wisdom of such things but by Christ who is in me

The Truth is only found in Christ Jesus
He is the way the truth and the life all else belongs to death which Christ had conquered.

HEARING THROUGH THE HOLY SPIRIT:

To all who have ears to hear let them hear with an empty mind and a receiving heat what the Holy Spirit speaks through me.

For those who do not think scripture is correct and the Word of God is designed to be read and understood by your own understanding:

the thing the Word of God is not something you read it is the living word by which you were given life and all creation was created

John 1:1-5 RV1885
In the beginning was the Word, and the Word was with God, and the Word was God. The same was in the beginning with God. All things were made by him; and without him was not anything made that hath been made. In him was life; and life was the light of men. And the light shineth in the darkness; and the darkness apprehended it not.

See the reason the world is not seeing and hearing the Word which is in all of us from before we were born is because it is the Holy Spirit that reads it to you it is a spiritual word prophetic and only understood in the language it was written in and that language is from God and translated by the Holy Spirit through the men and women who wrote it on paper it is

Coded by God to be heard by those who seek to know Him and ask the Holy spirit to intercede and make Christ their life.

Gods Will
But it is not I that knows this; it is from The Holy Spirit that you can only see the truth in Christ. You are confused and searching for answers from a world that has lied to you, and it sucks I know this very well and for a long time I went through the doubt and research

It is completely human to do this, and the devil knows this and the world we live in is His and He expects you to dig and research and make human sense of things this is the trick.

See God knew this from the beginning it is why He gave those who believe in Him the Gift of the Holy spirit knowing that all will be deceived without it.

No one will not be deceived at many times in their life this I guarantee

But with the Holy Spirit and looking, walking, and waiting on Christ Jesus will keep you from any deception that comes.

Truth is in Christ given to you From God by the Holy Spirit. Nothing can deceive what they do not see or understand

Proverbs 3:7-8
Be not wise in thine own eyes: Fear the LORD and depart from evil. It shall be healthy to thy navel, And marrow to thy bones.

BURDENSOME:

I write this with a heavy heart as yesterday was a battle of massive spiritual battles not so much that I struggled other than to let the Holy Spirit Guide my speech in text

Knowing that amid giving that water to those thirsty for a drink I myself would most likely spill the cup before I arrived to who needed it. We become so clumsy when we want to share the good news of salvation with others that we forget the work we are doing is not for God. It is
(HIS WORK.) That is being done through us.

2 Timothy 3:1-5
But mark this: There will be terrible times in the last days. People will be lovers of themselves, lovers of money, boastful, proud, abusive, disobedient to their parents, ungrateful, unholy, without love, unforgiving, slanderous, without self-control, brutal, not lovers of the good, treacherous, rash, conceited, lovers of pleasure rather than lovers of God– having a form of godliness but denying its power. Have nothing to do with such people.

TROUBLE:

I witnessed great confusion and frustration and then some anger and some very real evils in spirit and in flesh

Yesterday brought great sadness and overly concerning troubles that are very real in these days as we are taught by the word that would become evident in the last days. We must remain fixated on Christ as never before and continue at all times to be diligent in prayer and with all importance in growing and pulling close to us the Faith that we have in our Lord and Savior.

2 Timothy 3:6-7
They are the kind who worm their way into homes and gain control over gullible women, who are loaded down with sins and are swayed by all kinds of evil desires, always learning but never able to come to a knowledge of the truth.

I am saying these things not I but the spirit in me out of a sense of urgency that at times I do not comprehend to bring to you a sense of fear but one of urgency and assuredness to be steadfast in Faith and to allow The Holy Spirit to produce a love in you that nothing may turn from that love that only our Father can supply

2 Timothy 3:8-9
Just as Jannes and Jambres opposed Moses, so also these teachers oppose the truth. They are men of depraved minds,

who, as far as the faith is concerned, are rejected. But they will not get far because, as in the case of those men, their folly will be clear to everyone. Let words of malice towards you brothers and sisters be like a fine dust that just passes by without sticking for we know that the toils will come with a fierceness at times and only to cause you to lose hope

But our hope comes by faith in what is not seen for who can take away that which they do not know.

2 Timothy 3:12-17
In fact, everyone who wants to live a godly life in Christ Jesus will be persecuted, while evildoers and impostors will go from bad to worse, deceiving and being deceived. But as for you, continue in what you have learned and have become convinced of, because you know those from whom you learned it, and how from infancy you have known the Holy Scriptures, which are able to make you wise for salvation through faith in Christ Jesus. All Scripture is God-breathed and is useful for teaching, rebuking, correcting, and training in righteousness, so that the servant of God may be thoroughly equipped for every good work.

SUNRISE:

Today another sunrise closer to the Front gates of the Kingdom we are called back to let us rejoice and praise Him for all things great and small struggles and victories

Losses and pain let His name be Glorified in all the Earth and let us sing to the heavenly places so that the saints and angels alike may hear us.

To God our Father be all The Glory all the Power and all the Wisdom forever and ever Amen Amen Amen my soul rejoices in the warmth of His love for us. Please I insist go to a quiet place and read aloud this passage by Isaiah

As loud as you can muster and let the Lord of Hosts fill your soul and all who hear it. Be Glory and Honor and Power in His Holy name.

Isaiah 26:4-21 NASB1995
Trust in the Lord forever, For in God the Lord, we have an everlasting Rock. For He has brought low those who dwell on high, the unassailable city; He lays it low, He lays it low to the ground, He casts it to the dust. The foot will trample it, The feet of the afflicted, the steps of the helpless." The way of the righteous is smooth; O Upright One, make the path of the righteous level.

Indeed, while following the way of Your judgments, O Lord, we have waited for You eagerly.

Your name, even Your memory, is the desire of our souls. At night, my soul longs for You, indeed, my spirit within me seeks You diligently; For when the earth experiences Your judgments The inhabitants of the world learn righteousness. Though the wicked is shown favor, He does not learn righteousness; He deals unjustly in the land of uprightness and does not perceive the majesty of the Lord. O Lord, your hand is lifted, yet they do not see it. They see Your zeal for the people and are put to shame; Indeed, fire will devour Your enemies. Lord, you will establish peace for us Since You have also performed for us all our works. O Lord our God, other masters besides You have ruled us; But through You alone we confess Your name. The dead will not live, the departed spirits will not rise; Therefore, you have punished and destroyed them, And You have wiped out all remembrance of them. You have increased the nation, O Lord, you have increased the nation, you are glorified; You have extended all the borders of the land. O Lord, they sought You in distress; They could only whisper a prayer, your chastening was upon them. As the pregnant woman approaches the time to give birth, she writhes and cries out in her labor pains, thus were we before You, O Lord. We were pregnant, we writhed in labor, we gave birth, as it seems, only to wind. We could not accomplish deliverance for the earth, nor were inhabitants of the world born. Your dead will live; Their corpses will rise. You who lie in the dust, awake and shout for joy, for your dew is as the dew of the dawn, And the earth will give birth to the departed spirits. Come, my people, enter into your rooms and close your doors behind you; Hide for a little while Until indignation runs its course. For behold, the Lord is about to come out from His place to punish the inhabitants of the earth for their iniquity; And the earth will reveal her bloodshed and will no longer cover her slain.

For in this time many will be deceived not those who have chosen to follow Christ but those who follow the knowledge of the worldly treasures ...

But yet there will come yet a great deception one that has never come nor ever will be in all creation ... this one will offer all things of wealth and prosperity and health and knowledge to all men great and small rich and poor

For all will be deceived even the elect, if possible, this calls for wisdom not of yourself or the knowledge of the bible but only that which is given by the Holy Spirit in Christ Jesus our Lord and Savior.

Be not concerned of the things that will be offered as they are not the riches of heavenly things but no, they are of the world that God Almighty will bring to destruction in a single day.

For we should be only concerned on growing closer to Him and pulling all who we see out of the flames

I in vision not I but what is shown to me all those walking home to be with our Father through the valley of death tromping through guts and bones of the evils of Satan those horrible things that are grotesque and abominations to God

And as we walk the crowd of us marching is saying loud and in great voices ye though I walk through the valley of the shadows of death I will fear no evil...as we continue to hear the screams and torment of those sickly creatures and smell the rotting corpses, we hold out our hands and begin to pull those who reach for us from the flames that are the flames of God's wrath brought down on all that is wicked ... and we continue...your rod and your staff they comfort me ... thou doest prepare a table for me in the presence of my enemies...

And we come together and help heal those who have been wounded by their unbelief...Again all with loud resounding voices ...

Thou hast anointed my head with oil my cup overflows

SURELY GOODNESS AND LOVINGKINDNESS WILL FOLLOW ME ALL THE DAYS OF MY LIFE

...AND I WILL DWELL IN THE HOUSE OF THE LORD FOREVER AND EVER AMEN.

MAKE ME A CANDLE:

Make me a candle. Father.
When I strive to be a beacon.
Work in me to take away the painful glare. Dull the searing brightness.
So that I may draw close to those in need. Make me bearable.

And yet.
Keep me from growing dim so that I cast no light upon the way.
I seek to serve You.
Father.
And in doing so serve the ones I love. I cannot serve if I have no flame.

A candle I would be.

FATHER-
Bright enough to point the way.
Soft enough to soothe those tear-filled eyes who look to me to find Your Word. Your love.

Set Your flame within me ...
Make me a candle for Your glory.

WORTHY OF PRAISE:

My heart is in anguish this morning not because I am a disabled veteran and lost many.

But because the world is focused on Veterans Day to honor Soldiers for their sacrifice to a country that has turned their backs to God.

And although we live in this world the world is run by the evil Spirits not of flesh and blood. And all things done in the world for the world by the world's desires, even if done valiantly spoken of good intentions and for gain of self-praise or admiration. Is all done in vain and brings no Glory or Honor or Praise to our Father who is the One God of all things under heaven and earth.

For all you prideful Patriots that love their country so much and are willing to fight against tyranny and the things you have been taught to believe will bring you freedom. I, not I but Christ within me through the Holy Spirit ask you to go to prayer and seek wisdom from the Holy Spirit for what you should be giving your energy and time to throughout this day and every day.

If you give up your life for anything other than Christ Jesus, you have given your life to the sins of the world.

And for all of those fighting for the freedom of a country that has given you over to evil.

I, not I but Christ who lives in me through the Holy Spirit He implores you to hear the last words of this scripture and heed them to your heart. If you are fighting, it is not for the Glory of God, it is of selfish intent for your freedom for your glory and praise.

For in such things the word of God speaks of be not of boastfulness and pride in earthly things for all that is not of God and created for His Glory will go to destruction.

Ephesians 6:12 NASB
For our struggle is not against flesh and blood, but against the rulers, against the powers, against the world forces of this darkness,
against the spiritual forces of wickedness in the heavenly places.))

Today on a day of praise for fleshly sacrifice let us turn our eyes back to the ultimate sacrifice, The one that gave us life by conquering death itself is the only one by which we have salvation from all sin.

THE KING OF KINGS
THE LORD OF LORDS
CHRIST JESUS.

CHRISTS COMMANDMENTS TO US:

Commandments of God
And the signing of His Laws and Prophecy by Christ Jesus through the death and resurrection for all the sins of the world that all would not perish for eternity but have Everlasting life for those who choose to believe in Him.

(And He said to him, "'You shall love the Lord your God with all your heart, and with all your soul, and with all your mind.' This is the great and foremost commandment. Matthew 22:37-38)

Heart/Soul/Mind

3 parts of your human body you are told to love The Lord your God with, and this is not possible to do without first being taught by the Holy Spirit on how to love from the heart and soul, we can only love with the mind and even that we do not do well.

In order for us to be taught by the Holy Spirit we must first receive the Holy Spirit, and this requires us to Ask for help from Him and give up our life of the flesh and self-pride for the one of the Spirit and putting God before all else.

(The second is like it, 'You shall love your neighbor as yourself.' On these two commandments depend on the whole Law and the Prophets." Matthew 22:39-40)

Now if we have not learned how to follow the first commandment then there is no way possible you will come close to following the second commandment.

(Do you love everyone God created the same as yourself?)

(If yes, ask yourself if someone smashed your car window out would you give him a hug afterwards and forgive him?)

If no, then you have failed the second commandment.

So, to have this kind of love it is not just something we can do by our own standards we need the Wisdom and teachings of Christ taught to us by the Holy Spirit who intercedes in matters of the heart and soul that we do not know how to use.

"Do not think that I came to abolish the Law or the Prophets; I did not come to abolish but to fulfill. For truly I say to you, until heaven and earth pass away, not the smallest letter or stroke shall pass from the Law until all is accomplished. Whoever then (annuls) one of the least of these commandments, and teaches others to do the same, shall be called least in the kingdom of heaven; but whoever keeps and teaches them, he shall be called great in the kingdom of heaven. "For I say to you that unless your righteousness surpasses that of the scribes and Pharisees, you will not enter the kingdom of heaven. Matthew 5:17-20

Woe to whoever annuls (changes)the least of one of these commandments

(Fulfillment of the Laws)
(Matthew 5:21- Matthew 7:27)
These are the Beatitudes
Christ Jesus teachings that we are to abide by.

But He answered and said, "It is written, 'Man shall not live on bread alone, but on every word that proceeds out of the mouth of God.'" Matthew 4:4

Every word of God must be heard not by just reading it and trying to understand it in your mind

GOD'S Word is spoken, and we receive it from the Holy Spirit, and this is how we talk with our Father

Be careful to not mix your understanding of what the scriptures mean and what God is speaking to you.

We do not know what God means when we read it; it must be Spoken to us through the Holy Spirit only then do we comprehend what our Father is saying.

Abide in Me, and I in you. As the branch cannot bear fruit of itself unless it abides in the vine, so neither can you unless you abide in Me. I am the vine, you are the branches; he who abides in Me and I in him, he bears much fruit, for apart from Me you can do nothing. If anyone does not abide in Me, he is thrown away as a branch and dries up; and they gather them and cast them into the fire and they are burned. If you abide in Me, and My words abide in you, ask whatever you wish, and it will be done for you. My Father is glorified by this, that you bear much fruit, and so prove to be My disciples. Just as the Father has loved Me, I have also loved you; abide in My love. If you keep My commandments, you will abide in My love; just as I have kept My Father's commandments and abide in His love. These

things I have spoken to you so that My joy may be in you, and that your joy may be made full.
John 15:4-11

NEED VS WANT/ WHAT VS WHY

Stop and ask yourself
These questions today as an individual and how do you feel about it.

1) what do you WANT to know today?

2 (what do you NEED to know today?

3 (how will knowing, whatever IT is bring you peace and knowledge

And the peace of God, which surpasses all understanding, will guard your hearts and your minds in Christ Jesus. What you have learned and received and heard and seen in me–practice these things, and the God of peace will be with you.
Philippians 4:7

Finally, brothers, whatever is true, whatever is honorable, whatever is just, whatever is pure, whatever is lovely, whatever is commendable, if there is any excellence, if there is anything worthy of praise, think about these things.
Philippians 4:8

Choosing a life in Christ you will no longer need to know WHAT is happening because the Holy Spirit will show you WHY.

But seek first His kingdom and His righteousness, and all these things will be added to you. "So do not worry about tomorrow; for tomorrow will care for itself. Each day has enough trouble of its own.
Matthew 6:33

WORRY:

(Everyday a new worry, every moment a new fear, but the Son of king David, Solomon, explains in great detail these things we call NEW and worrisome)

The words of the Preacher, the son of David, king in Jerusalem. "Vanity of vanities," says the Preacher, "Vanity of vanities! All is vanity." What advantage does man have in all his work Which he does under the sun? A generation goes and a generation comes, But the earth remains forever. Also, the sun rises and the sun sets; And hastening to its place it rises there again. Blowing toward the south, then turning toward the north, the wind continues swirling along; And on its circular courses the wind returns. All the rivers flow into the sea, Yet the sea is not full. To the place where the rivers flow, there they flow again. All things are wearisome; Man is not able to tell it. The eye is not satisfied with seeing, nor is the ear filled with hearing. That which has been that which will be, and that which has been done is that which will be done. So, there is nothing new under the sun. Is there anything of which one might say, "See this, it is new"? Already it has existed for ages Which were before us. There is no remembrance of earlier things; And, of the later things which will occur, there will be for them no remembrance Among those who will come later still. Ecclesiastes 1:1-11 NASB

(I implore you all brothers and sisters not I but Christ in me by the Holy Spirit to be only fixated on things of Heaven and in prayer and supplication to the Lord not to be entangled in the comings and goings of things the way the world does but to think on only things which give Glory to The Father by in doing so you will be made ready for all which will come against the world and have peace amidst the chaos and confusion)

(King Solomon's son of King David)
I, the Preacher, have been king over Israel in Jerusalem. And I set my mind to seek and explore by wisdom concerning all that has been done under heaven. It is a grievous task which God has given to the sons of men to be afflicted with. I have seen all the works which have been done under the sun, and behold, all is vanity and striving after wind. What is crooked cannot be straightened and what is lacking cannot be counted. I said to myself, "Behold, I have magnified and increased wisdom more than all who were over Jerusalem before me; and my mind has observed a wealth of wisdom and knowledge." And I set my mind to know wisdom and to know madness and folly; I realized that this also is striving after wind. Because in much wisdom there is much grief and increasing knowledge results in increasing pain. Ecclesiastes 1:12-18 NASB

(We are not to be concerned as the world is concerned for, we know that all things are accomplished according to our Fathers Will and

And all prophecies will be fulfilled according to the Word of God.

Nothing in the news, on tv, on the internet, in social media, or from any man on this planet is God's Truth.)

JESUS IS...
THE WAY,
THE TRUTH, and THE LIFE.

(If you want the inside scoop on how this all ends and why things are happening, I guarantee you will not hear it with your ears or see it with your eyes. It is only available through Christ and given to all who seek Him by the Holy Spirit which is all of God's Wisdom and Truth and Grace and Peace and Love.)

Be anxious for nothing, but in everything by prayer and supplication with thanksgiving let your requests be made known to God. And the peace of God, which surpasses all comprehension, will guard your hearts and your minds in Christ Jesus. Finally, brethren, whatever is true, whatever is honorable, whatever is right, whatever is pure, whatever is lovely, whatever is of good repute, if there is any excellence and if anything, worthy of praise, dwell on these things. The things you have learned, received, and heard and seen in me, practice these things, and the God of peace will be with you. Philippians 4:6-9 NASB

(If you are entangled in the problem of the things going on you will surely become tired and weary from all of it and will find no resolve or peace in any of it.)

"I say to you, my friends, do not be afraid of those who kill the body and after that have no more that they can do. But I will warn you whom to fear, fear the One who, after He has killed, has authority to cast into hell; yes, I tell you, fear Him! Are not five sparrows sold for two cents? Yet not one of them is forgotten before God. Indeed, the very hairs of your head are all numbered. Do not fear; you are more valuable than many sparrows. Luke 12:4-7 NASB

1)LOVE the Lord your God with all your HEART, with all your SOUL and with all your MIND. (If your mind is on the worries of the world how can your mind be on loving the Lord?) (What you think on and speak about there your heart will be also and when it is not of loving God you will surely be deceived.)

2)LOVE your NEIGHBOR as yourself.

(You cannot Love like God, it is impossible without Christ and the Holy Spirit to do.)

Would you embrace an enemy who physically beat you with no ill intended thoughts towards him?

Therefore, Jesus calls us to Love God first because if we Choose with our MIND to love God the Holy Spirit teaches us how to Love God's way with our HEART AND SOUL.

Then we through the Holy Spirit can love others with a deeper love that is only available to those who choose to receive it.

He who has ears let him hear what the Holy Spirit is speaking to our hearts today Father and let us sing praises to you Father for by Your Grace we are Saved through Faith in Christ Jesus.

GOD'S WORD RECEIVED:

Speaking in tongues / receiving of parables
This is in reference to the Holy Spirit directing and guiding your speech.

Jesus taught and spoke in tongues and parables to all who would receive Him and listen with an inner ear of the Spirit as this is the only way to hear the Word of God.

(At that time Jesus said, "I praise You, Father, Lord of heaven and earth, that You have hidden these things from the wise and intelligent and have revealed them to infants.)

The Holy Spirit is the Helper, translator, He is the voice of the Word of God spoken and received by the heart and soul of those who receive Christ fully to take the place of who they are and be born a new creation of Christ alive in them and them dead to self.

(Crucified to all matters of the world knowing that all things past present and future are done by God's Will and all prophecy of God will be fulfilled.) Those today like the pharisees and priests of old are the ones that have much knowledge of scripture and are very wise in their own eyes, but no man has Wisdom of God, and we don't attain God's Wisdom The Holy Spirit is all

Wisdom of God and it is by the Holy Spirit that all things are accomplished through us not by us.

When we die to self and our own understanding we become an infant of our new life in Christ And begin in Faith as a child, and as a child we require instruction and teaching in this new way and it is only done by Christ Jesus and re taught to us through the Holy Spirit and by the Holy Spirit we now do not speak as the world speak or of things pertaining to the world, we now have ears to hear what God says and we receive from the Holy Spirit in scriptures and prophecies spoken by God.(he who has ears let him what the Holy Spirit says.

(Yes, Father, for this way was well-pleasing in Your sight. All things have been handed over to
Me by My Father; and no one knows the Son except the Father; nor does anyone know the
Father except the Son, and anyone to whom the Son wills to reveal Him.)

Only through Christ the Son do we know God and only God knows the Son and as we receive Christ, He makes us known to God and we receive the Holy Spirit so that we may now be taught by Christ and from Christ we are received by the father.

("Come to Me, all who are weary and heavy-laden, and I will give you rest. Take My yoke upon you and LEARN FROM ME, for I am gentle and humble in heart, and you will find rest for your souls. For My yoke is easy and My burden is light.") Matthew 11:25-30

(LEARN FROM ME)

When we are born a new creation in Christ our only teacher is Christ Jesus and received by the Holy Spirit and placed in us as we grow and learn the ways of a life not one of self but of Christ alive in us as we are now born again.

BE NOT OF THE WORLD:

1 John 2:15-29 NASB
Do not love the world (nor the things in the world).

Ask yourself what you search for everyday?
What do you talk about with others?
What do you spend your time thinking about?

(If anyone loves the world, the love of the Father is not in him.)
Love is something we devote all our time to.

(For all that is in the world, the lust of the flesh and the lust of the eyes and the boastful pride of life, is not from the Father, but is from the world.)

Pride of self, pride of country
Patriotism, Q, any Allegiance to any one or thing is an idol and all the world. Even using scripture for the gain of being right is self-loathing and a sin.

(The world is passing away, and also its lusts;)

(But the one who does the will of God lives forever. Children, it is the last hour; and just as you heard that antichrist is coming, even now many antichrists have appeared; from this we know that it is the last hour.)

Once the 1st beast falls
Then the prophecy of Abomination of Desolation is complete.
This is the destruction of one evil by the other evil.
(Daniel 11)

(They went out from us, but they were not really of us; for if they had been of us, they would have remained with us; but they went out, so that it would be shown that they all are not of us.

(Psalms 23:5a)
Thou dost prepare a table in the presence of my enemy

(Psalms 78:19)
Then they spoke against God, they said God can prepare a table in the wilderness?

(But you have an anointing from the Holy One, and you all know. I have not written to you because you do not know the truth, but because you do know it, and because no lie is the truth.)

(Psalms 23:5b)
Thou hast anointed my head with oil, my cup overflows.

(Psalms 16:5)
The Lord is the portion of my inheritance and my cup overflows.

All things of the world have no truth, only lies and confusion.

(Who is the liar but the one who denies that Jesus is the Christ? This is the antichrist, the one who denies the Father and the Son.)

He will rise like a Phoenix from the ashes and will hate both sides of evil and even curse all that they did and will gain all adoration and perform great things that the world has never seen.

(Revelation 17:10-11) and they are seven kings; five have fallen, one is, the other has not yet come; and when he comes, he must remain a little while. The beast which was and is not, is himself also an eighth and is one of the seven, and he goes to destruction.

(Whoever denies the Son does not have the Father); He will expect all to worship him.

(The one who confesses the Son has the Father also.)
(As for you, let that abide in you which you heard from the beginning. If what you heard from the beginning abides in you, you also will abide in the Son and in the Father. This is the promise which He Himself made to us: eternal life.)

These things I have written to you concerning those who are trying to deceive you. As for you, the anointing which you received from Him abides in you, and you have no need for anyone to teach you; but as His anointing teaches you about all things, and is true and is not a lie, and just as it has taught you, you abide in Him. Now, little children abide in Him, so that when He appears, we may have confidence and not shrink away from Him in shame at His coming. If you know that He is righteous, you know that everyone also who practices righteousness is born of Him.

Be alert for the days of great deception are yet to come

Therefore, I urge you, brethren, by the mercies of God, to present your bodies a living and holy sacrifice, acceptable to

God, which is your spiritual service of worship. And do not be conformed to this world, but be transformed by the renewing of your mind, so that you may prove what the will of God is, that which is good, acceptable, and perfect. For through the grace given to me I say to everyone among you not to think more highly of himself than he ought to think; but to think so as to have sound judgment, as God has allotted to each a measure of faith. Romans 12:1-3 NASB

Bless those who persecute you; bless and do not curse. Rejoice with those who rejoice, and weep with those who weep. Be of the same mind toward one another; do not be haughty in mind but associate with the lowly. Do not be wise in your own estimation.

Romans 12:14-16 NASB

BELIEF V.S. FAITH:

Belief

Definition of belief

1: A state or habit of mind in which trust or confidence is placed in some person or thing Faith

1. An allegiance to duty or a person

In the days before the crucifixion and resurrection man had belief in God as He had not sent Himself (spirit of Christ) into the world to save the world from sin. people saw God and God spoke to them.
So, they had (belief) in God.

In this world we live in we were born after the days of the death and resurrection of Jesus (all Man/all God in the flesh) and for this reason we are saved from death if we choose to live for Him as He died so that we may have life not by our works but because of Jesus.

Christ= Spirit of God
Jesus= Holy Spirit of God in the flesh.

And through the gift of the Holy Spirit, we can communicate with God directly through the Holy Spirit of God who is Christ (Holy Spirit) in us.

(John 14:26)
But the Helper, the Holy Spirit, whom the Father will send in My name, He will teach you all things, and bring to your remembrance all that I said to you.

And
Because we do not see or hear God like in the days before Jesus (son of God) son of man) (God in the Flesh)
What the world has is called belief in God
What we who have been born a new creation in Christ Jesus it is called (Faith).

(Hebrews 11:1)
Now faith is the assurance of things hoped for, the conviction of things not seen.

For now, we being born again
Live by faith we need not be concerned with the world's views or its quarreling.

(1 John 2:15-17)
Do not love the world nor the things in the world. If anyone loves the world, the love of the Father is not in him. For all that is in the world, the lust of the flesh and the lust of the eyes and the boastful pride of life, is not from the Father, but is from the world. The world is passing away, and also its lusts; but the one who does the will of God lives forever.

But we are now under a new law and a life that is not pleasing to self but to God who by Grace has given us all things according to His Will.

(2 Corinthians 5:7) for we walk by faith, not by sight.

(Romans 5:1-5)
Since we have been justified by faith, we have peace with God through our Lord Jesus Christ. Through him we have also obtained access by faith into this grace in which we stand, and we rejoice in [hope] of the glory of God. Not only that, but we rejoice in our sufferings, knowing that suffering produces endurance, and endurance produces character, and character produces hope, and hope does not put us to shame, because God's love has been poured into our hearts through the Holy Spirit who has been given to us.

Because we are of the Spirit we are to live by the fruit of the Spirit.

(Galatians 5:22-26)
But the fruit of the Spirit is love, joy, peace, patience, kindness, goodness, faithfulness, gentleness, self-control; against such things there is no law. And those who belong to Christ Jesus have crucified the flesh with its passions and desires. If we live by the Spirit, let us also keep in step with the Spirit. Let us not become conceited, provoking one another, envying one another.

See we live in the world
And the world had its laws of old before Christ.

But we are born of the Spirit after Christ so the laws of God which are made by the Spirit of God who lives in us are the only laws that apply to us as we are made whole by Christ in us.

We must first BELIEVE
That God sent His Son as Himself in the Spirit to be born in the flesh (JESUS) die in the flesh (JESUS)
Conquer all death, even the death of eternal hell, to save us from sin. And that both the flesh of Jesus (man)
And the Spirit within the flesh rose from the grave to be with the Father.

(1 John 4:17)
By this is love perfected with us, so that we may have confidence for the day of judgment, because as he is so also, we are in this world.

(Ephesians 2:1-10)
And you were dead in your trespasses and sins, in which you formerly walked according to the course of this world, according to the prince of the power of the air, of the spirit that is now working in the sons of disobedience. Among them we too all formerly lived in the lusts of our flesh, indulging the desires of the flesh and of the mind, and were by nature children of wrath, even as the rest. But God, being rich in mercy, because of His great love with which He loved us, even when we were dead in our transgressions, made us alive together with Christ (by grace you have been saved), and raised us up with Him, and seated us with Him in the heavenly places in Christ Jesus, so that in the ages to come He might show the surpassing riches of His grace in kindness toward us in Christ Jesus. For by grace, you have been saved through faith; and that not of yourselves, it is the gift of God; not as a result of works, so that no one may boast. For we are His workmanship, created in Christ Jesus for good works, which God prepared beforehand so that we would walk in them.

THE GREAT RESET:

When anyone who follows the term Great Reset the first thing, they get tied up in is the addiction that every human being on the plan IT has is MONEY.

1 Timothy 6:9-10
But those who desire to be rich fall into temptation, into a snare, into many senseless and harmful desires that plunge people into ruin and destruction. For the love of money is a root of all kinds of evils. It is through this craving that some have wandered away from the faith and pierced themselves with many pangs.

However, the reset that is happening is not one of money but of all things that are not given life by Christ and created by the only God of the heavens and earth. It is a reset of all creation

Ridding the world of the world's desires.

Luke 12:49-56
"I came to cast fire on the earth and would that it was already kindled! I have a baptism to be baptized with, and how great is my distress until it is accomplished! Do you think that I have come to give peace on earth? No, I tell you, but rather division. For from now on in one house there will be five divided, three against two and two against three. They will be divided, father against son and son against father, mother against daughter and daughter against mother, mother-in-law against

her daughter-in-law and daughter-in-law against mother-in-law." He also said to the crowds, "When you see a cloud rising in the west, you say at once, 'A shower is coming.' And so, it happens. And when you see the south wind blowing, you say, 'There will be scorching heat,' and it happens. You hypocrites! You know how to interpret the appearance of earth and sky, but why do you not know how to interpret the present time?

Those in positions of power will be used to usher in the manifestations of evil and the things of the world not created by God and given life by Christ.

All the things created by man that go against the laws of God and the 2 commandments of Christ (1) And he said to him, "You shall love the Lord your God with all your heart and with all your soul and with all your mind. (2) And a second is like it: You shall love your neighbor as yourself. On these two commandments hangeth the whole law (10 commandments), and the prophets (laws of Moses). All most of these will be brought before the wrath of God.

Wheat (God's creation) and weeds (things not of God or the fruit if the spirit

Matthew 13:24-30
He put another parable before them, saying, "The kingdom of heaven may be compared to a man who sowed good seed in his field, but while his men were sleeping, his enemy came and sowed weeds among the wheat and went away. So, when the plants came up and bore grain, then the weeds appeared also. And the servants of the master of the house came and said to him, 'Master, did you not sow good seed in your field? How then does it have weeds?' He said to them, 'An enemy has done this.' So, the servants said to him, 'Then do you want us to go and gather them?' But he said, 'No, lest in gathering the weeds you

root up the wheat along with them. Let both grow together until the harvest, and at harvest time I will tell the reapers, "Gather the weeds first and bind them in bundles to be burned but gather the wheat into my barn.""'

We are born of the Spirit of God and made whole by the Spirit of Christ who is in us.
We must not hold onto what is not of God as the laws of Moses and the two commandments state.

Ephesians 4:17-22, 24-25
Now this I say and testify in the Lord, that you must no longer walk as the Gentiles do, in the futility of their minds. They are darkened in their understanding, alienated from the life of God because of the ignorance that is in them, due to their hardness of heart. They have become callous and have given themselves up to sensuality, greedy to practice every kind of impurity. But that is not the way you learned Christ! – assuming that you have heard about him and were taught in him, as the truth is in Jesus, to put off your old self, which belongs to your former manner of life and is corrupt through deceitful desires, and to put on the new self, created after the likeness of God in true righteousness and holiness. Therefore, having put away falsehood, let each one of you speak the truth with his neighbor, for we are members one of another.

We must stay in faithfulness to Christ as all of this kind of living is the fruit of the Spirit.

Galatians 5:22-26
But the fruit of the Spirit is love, joy, peace, patience, kindness, goodness, faithfulness, gentleness, self-control; against such things there is no law. And those who belong to Christ Jesus have crucified the flesh with its passions and desires. If we live by the

Spirit, let us also keep in step with the Spirit. Let us not become conceited, provoking one another, envying one another.

We should be worshiping God by living as Jesus did as He is both the spirit of God and by who we are given life.

Romans 5:1-5
Therefore, since we have been justified by faith, we have peace with God through our Lord Jesus Christ. Through him we have also obtained access by faith into this grace in which we stand, and we rejoice in hope of the glory of God. Not only that, but we rejoice in our sufferings, knowing that suffering produces endurance, and endurance produces character, and character produces hope, and hope does not put us to shame, because God's love has been poured into our hearts through the Holy Spirit who has been given to us.

James 1:2-6, 12, 19-22
Count it all joy, my brothers, when you meet trials of various kinds, for you know that the testing of your faith produces steadfastness. And let steadfastness have its full effect, that you may be perfect and complete, lacking in nothing. If any of you lacks wisdom, let him ask God, who gives generously to all without reproach, and it will be given to him. But let him ask in faith, with no doubting, for the one who doubts is like a wave of the sea that is driven and tossed by the wind. Blessed is the man who remains steadfast under trial, for when he has stood the test he will receive the crown of life, which God has promised to those who love him. Know this, my beloved brothers: let every person be quick to hear, slow to speak, slow to anger; for the anger of man does not produce the righteousness of God. Therefore, put away all filthiness and rampant wickedness and receive with meekness the implanted word, which is able to save your souls. But be doers of the word, and not hearers only, deceiving yourselves.

Remember,
Love, Kindness and Humility is required of us as we are the light of life that the world will see.

2 Corinthians 6:2-10
For he says, "In a favorable time I listened to you, and in a day of salvation I have helped you." Behold, now is the favorable time; behold, now is the day of salvation. We put no obstacle in anyone's way, so that no fault may be found with our ministry, but as servants of God we commend ourselves in every way: by great endurance, in afflictions, hardships, calamities, beatings, imprisonments, riots, labors, sleepless nights, hunger; by purity, knowledge, patience, kindness, the Holy Spirit, genuine love; by truthful speech, and the power of God; with the weapons of righteousness for the right hand and for the left; through honor and dishonor, through slander and praise. We are treated as impostors, and yet are true; as unknown, and yet well known; as dying, and behold, we live; as punished, and yet not killed; as sorrowful, yet always rejoicing; as poor, yet making many rich; as having nothing, yet possessing everything.

BE LIKE CHRIST:

As we are called to Christ and given this new life, we must strive to be like Him, and one of the biggest obstacles is how to have humility.

Philippians 2:1-18 NASB
1)Therefore if there is any encouragement in Christ, if there is any consolation of love, if there is any fellowship of the Spirit, if any affection and compassion,

Make my joy complete by being of the same mind, maintaining the same love, united in spirit, intent on one purpose.

(The Holy Spirit is teaching us through Apostle Paul the attributes of what we, striving to be like Christ should all have and also, we should all be on the same page with a character of encouragement to whoever we meet and to be consoling in love, to fellowship and be guided by the Holy Spirit in joy and to have affection to all people as they also are just as precious in the eyes of our Father as you are.)

3)Do nothing from selfishness or empty conceit, but with humility of mind regard one another as more important than yourselves.

(No one in the world is any better than another, Christ Jesus is the Lord of Lords for all people in the same way)

4) do not merely look out for your own personal interests, but also for the interests of others.

(Those who are strong in faith need to be the strength for others but without regarding Himself as any better than the person they are helping.)

5)Have this attitude in yourselves which was also in Christ Jesus, who, although He existed in the form of God, did not regard equality with God a thing to be grasped, but emptied Himself, taking the form of a bondservant, and being made in the likeness of men.

Being found in appearance as a man, He humbled Himself by becoming obedient to the point of death, even death on a cross.

(Jesus Christ the Son of God was born in the same way as you and I were, He was also in the Image of God Himself but Jesus never regarded Himself to be an equal to God, He considered Himself just like you and I. Obedient and a Servant to all of God's Commandments and to all people he met in everything He did. He was so obedient that He completely disregarded Himself as anything worthy of praise even willing to sacrifice Himself for the sins and faults of everyone on earth, past present and future, and The Father was so pleased with Him, He

Gave Him the name above all Names)

6)For this reason also, God highly exalted Him, and bestowed on Him the name, which is above every name, so that at the name of Jesus every knee will bow, of those who are in heaven and on earth and under the earth, and that every tongue will confess that Jesus Christ is Lord, to the glory of God the Father.

7) Work out your salvation with fear and trembling; for it is God who is at work in you, both to will and to work for His good pleasure.

(We should every day in every situation think act and respond just as if God is standing right next to you and judging everything you are doing, saying, and thinking because He is)

8) Do all things without grumbling or disputing; so that you will prove yourselves to be blameless and innocent, children of God above reproach in the midst of a crooked and perverse generation, among whom you appear as lights in the world, holding fast the word of life,

(In all areas of your life, the good, the bad and the worst, be not a complainer, do not even complain to yourself in private for the inward thoughts of a man will become the outward actions he displays.)

(Ever hear the term you are what you eat? Well, more importantly you become what you think, garbage in garbage out, others will see who you are by what you display and what you display comes from the heart and put there by what we think. We are to be the light of Christ and to do that we must always consider ourselves as less than everyone we meet, this is the Definition of Humility,

9) I rejoice and share my joy with you all. You too, I urge you, rejoice in the same way and share your joy with me.

(Our constant growth in Christ will bring us Constant Joy unimaginable happiness and as we remain blameless in the eyes of the Lord, He finds great pleasure in our happiness to serve others first,

To not grumble or complain about what He calls us to do and to always be guided by the Holy Spirit in all our thoughts and feelings and therefore guide others back to Christ simply by us being humble and obedient, and putting Christ as the front and center in all we are.)
Philippians 2:1-18 NASB

TESTING OF THE SPIRIT AND DISCERNMENT OF THE HOLY SPIRIT:

I understand that all will not be at the same understanding of God's Word as I wish only the Fathers Will be done

I have chosen to live a crucified life to bear not only my cross but to guide others to find theirs having put all self to death that I may be of full service to my Father

Let us not be confused by our own understanding or by the teachings of those not of the Spirit.

Beloved, do not believe every spirit, but test the spirits to see whether they are from God, because many false prophets have gone out into the world. By this you know the Spirit of God: every spirit that confesses that Jesus Christ has come in the flesh is from God; and every spirit that does not confess Jesus is not from God; this is the spirit of the antichrist, of which you have heard that it is coming, and now it is already in the world. 1 John 4:1-3

An example of Man's teaching by their interpretation.:
Not by intentionally doing so but by not receiving the Word of God through the Holy Spirit.

They are deaf and when a word is spoken without the Spirits Guidance it becomes deceitful.

(The trinity is manufactured religion)

The trinity is not manufactured religion it is man's own understanding of the Spirit of God and the Son of God and the Holy Spirit
For these three are separate in being yet they agree all together as the Spirit of God
The Spirit of Christ
The Holy Spirit are one in agreement in Spirit.

This is the One who came by water and blood, Jesus Christ, not with the water only, but with the water and with the blood. It is the Spirit who testifies because the Spirit is the truth. For there are three that testify: the Spirit and the water and the blood; and the three agree. 1 John 5:6-8 NASB

Thank me not for all I write but thank Christ as He created in me what you see. I want nothing more in life than for all who read these to hear Christ calling them home to Him for if I shall pass away His love remains the light that all have seen in me for, I am just a servant and tool for the ministry of our Father's Will.

SEARCH ME:

(Father, my heart aches and my soul is hurting today, so many have forgotten who they are and how wonderfully made they are. I bring this to you Father as you hear my cries and know my pain. For what I feel I cannot put to words, so as always Lord when words fail me, may You speak.)

O Lord, you have searched me and known me. You know when I sit down and when I rise up; You understand my thoughts from afar. You scrutinize my path and my lying down and are intimately acquainted with all my ways. Even before there is a word on my tongue, Behold, O Lord, you know it all. You have enclosed me behind and before and laid Your hand upon me. Such knowledge is too wonderful for me; It is too high; I cannot attain to it.

Where can I go from Your Spirit? Or where can I flee from Your presence? If I ascend to heaven, you are there; If I make my bed in Sheol, behold, you are there. If I take the wings of the dawn, If I dwell in the remotest part of the sea, even there Your hand will lead me, and your right hand will lay hold of me. If I say, "Surely the darkness will overwhelm me, And the light around me will be night," Even the darkness is not dark to You, And the night is as bright as the day. Darkness and light are alike to You.

(Take our vision away Father that we might be blind to all. We are shown a detestable world of anxiety, worry, doubt, fear, self-gratification, pride of self, pride of life, pride of country.

For none of these things are from you Lord.

Make us Deaf Lord so as not to hear anything other than the beautiful sound of the Holy Spirit teaching us and guiding us in your Ways.)

For You formed my inward parts; You wove me in my mother's womb. I will give thanks to You, for I am fearfully and wonderfully made; Wonderful are Your works, and my soul knows it very well.

My frame was not hidden from You, When I was made in secret, and skillfully wrought in the depths of the earth.

Your eyes have seen my unformed substance.

And in Your book were all written the days that were ordained for me, when as yet there was not one of them.

How precious also are Your thoughts to me, O God!

How vast is the sum of them!
If I should count them, they would outnumber the sand. When I awake, I am still with You.

Search me, O God, and know my heart; Try me and know my anxious thoughts; And see if there be any hurtful way in me and lead me in the everlasting way. Psalms 139:1-18, 23-24 NASB

A NEW WAY:

(Father I have much concern for my brothers and sisters in Christ Jesus for the Holy Spirit has put a sight in my eyes of the wayward teachings of men that claim to be called by You. I question not Your Will Father for it is Your Will be done not mine. Just as in the days of old many are going to and from and conforming to a world of anxiety and worry Lord and leading others not to Your peace but one temporary in nature. Let them see the writing on their hearts Father and put away the false hope they seek in others and find Your everlasting Grace in a world of confusion and deception.)

Such confidence we have through Christ toward God. Not that we are adequate in ourselves to consider anything as coming from ourselves, but our adequacy is from God, who also made us adequate as servants of a new covenant, not of the letter but of the Spirit; for the letter kills, but the Spirit gives life.

(Let us see O Lord the letter written on our hearts that we may be lacking in nothing and be made available for Your work to be done through us not by us.)

But if the ministry of death, in letters engraved on stones, came with glory, so that the sons of Israel could not look intently at the face of Moses because of the glory of his face, fading as it was, how will the ministry of the Spirit fail to be even more with glory? For if the ministry of condemnation has glory, much more does the ministry of righteousness abound in glory.

(Let us know Your righteousness not our rightness for only through you is anything done that is done.)

For indeed what had glory, in this case has no glory because of the glory that surpasses it. For if that which fades away was with glory, much more that which remains is in glory.

Therefore, having such a hope, we use great boldness in our speech, and are not like Moses, who used to put a veil over his face so that the sons of Israel would not look intently at the end of what was fading away. But their minds were hardened; for until this very day at the reading of the old covenant the same veil remains unlifted, because it is removed in Christ. But to this day whenever Moses is read, a veil lies over their heart; but whenever a person turns to the Lord, the veil is taken away.

(Let us be the window to You Father and allow only the Holy Spirit to speak in our place that the new Covenant in Christ Jesus by which is written in us be on display for the world to see the MAJESTY AND POWER AND LOVE AND GRACE AND PEACE that can only be received from a deep and fully surrendering commitment to You.)

Now the Lord is the Spirit, and where the Spirit of the Lord is, there is liberty. But we all, with unveiled face, beholding as in a mirror the glory of the Lord, are being transformed into the same image from glory to glory, just as from the Lord, the Spirit. 2 Corinthians 3:1-18 NASB

NO FREEDOM OF THE WORLD:

Now we request you, brethren, with regard to the coming of our Lord Jesus Christ and our gathering together to Him, that you not be quickly shaken from your composure or be disturbed either by a spirit, a message, or a letter as if from us to the effect that the day of the Lord has come. Let no one in any way deceive you, for it will not come unless the apostasy comes first,

(APOSTASY:)
1) an act of refusing to continue to follow, obey, or recognize a religious faith

2) abandonment of a previous loyalty: DEFECTION

(Every day in my work and my connections with others I see others still holding on to all kinds of religious beliefs and the push and pull of all the religions claiming theirs is best. Whether it is Patriotism, Catholicism, Judaism,

Christian Theology, Mormon, etc. etc. etc. The Q following claims a one world Religion. There is only Christ Jesus.)

Romans 8:1-2 Therefore, there is now no condemnation for those who are in Christ Jesus. For the law of the Spirit of life in Christ Jesus has set you free from the law of sin and of death. and the man of lawlessness is revealed, the son of destruction, who opposes and exalts himself above every so-called god or object of worship, so that he takes his seat in the temple of God, displaying himself as being God.

(The one who exalts himself above every religion and every so-called god sits in the temple of God and claims to be God has not been shown yet but will be here is proof of prophecy coming to Fulfillment)

(THE CATHOLIC-MUSLIM INTERFAITH COUNCIL CREATED BY POPE FRANCIS
ANNOUNCES NEW CHRISLAM HEADQUARTERS OPENING IN 2022 THAT COMBINES A MOSQUE AND CHURCH ACCORDING TO SIGNED
COVENANT.) (https://believersportal.com/one-world-religion-headquarters-to-open-2022/)

Do you not remember that while I was still with you, I was telling you these things? And you know what restrains him now, so that in his time he will be revealed. For the mystery of lawlessness is already at work; only he who now restrains will do so until he is taken out of the way.

(Look around you in everything you encounter there has never been so much disarray globally ever in recorded history every land is portraying the mystery of lawlessness and the dark is being brought to light by the ones who will usher in the one world Religion and offer spectacular freedoms and claim victory over evil then from this will arise one.)

Then that lawless one will be revealed whom the Lord will slay with the breath of His mouth and bring to an end by the appearance of His coming; that is, the one whose coming is in accord with the activity of Satan, with all power and signs and false wonders, and with all the deception of wickedness for those who perish, because they did not receive the love of the truth so as to be saved.

(Seek first the Kingdom of God and all His Righteousness and all these will be added to you.
The Holy Spirit Will Guide you on the narrow path so to know His truth and to not be deceived.)

For this reason, God will send upon them a deluding influence so that they will believe what is false, in order that they all may be judged who did not believe the truth but took pleasure in wickedness. But we should always give thanks to God for you, brethren beloved by the Lord, because God has chosen you from the beginning for salvation through sanctification by the Spirit and faith in the truth. It was for this He called you through our gospel, that you may gain the glory of our Lord Jesus Christ.

So then, brethren, stand firm and hold to the traditions which you were taught, whether by word of mouth or by letter from us. Now may our Lord Jesus Christ Himself and God our Father, who has loved us and given us eternal comfort and good hope by grace, comfort and strengthen your hearts in every good work and word.

2 Thessalonians 2:1-17 NASB

(Our King is returning, and your Salvation is found in Christ Jesus not in a world of brokenness and lies and deceit you will get no peace from any other thing or person. There is no Freedom the world can offer you; it is only death they offer in disguise of Freedom and Prosperity.)

WEAKNESS:

(Let us not play the silly games of the world and say to ourselves or let the words come from our lips, oh I have done this or that that they speak of, or I have done it better and accomplished more. Are we all not slaves to a life of sin and all ruled by those who deny Christ, so who by any means can boast of such things, let us seal up our foolish mouths.)

Since many boasts according to the flesh, I will boast also. For you, being so wise, tolerate the foolish gladly. For you tolerate it if anyone enslaves you, anyone devours you, anyone takes advantage of you, anyone exalts himself, anyone hits you in the face. To my shame I must say that we have been weak by comparison. But in whatever respect anyone else is bold—I speak in foolishness—I am just as bold myself. Are they Hebrews? So am I. Are they Israelites? So am I. Are they descendants of Abraham? So am I. Are they servants of Christ? —I speak as if insane—I more so; in far more labors, in far more imprisonments, beaten times without number, often in danger of death. Five times I received from the Jews thirty-nine lashes. Three times I was beaten with rods, once I was stoned, three times I was shipwrecked, a night and a day I have spent in the deep. I have been on frequent journeys, in dangers from rivers, dangers from robbers, dangers from my countrymen, dangers from the Gentiles, dangers in the city, dangers in the wilderness, dangers on the sea, dangers among false brethren; I have been in labor and hardship, through many sleepless nights, in hunger and thirst, often without food, in cold and exposure. Apart from such external things, there is the daily pressure on me of concern for all the churches. Who is weak without my being weak? Who is led into sin without my intense concern? If I have to boast, I will boast of what pertains to my weakness. The God and Father of the Lord Jesus, He who is blessed forever, knows that I am not lying.

2 Corinthians 11:18-31 NASB

Boasting is necessary, though it is not profitable; but I will go on to visions and revelations of the Lord. I know a man in Christ who fourteen years ago–whether in the body I do not know, or out of the body I do not know, God knows–such a man was caught up to the third heaven. And I know how such a man–whether in the body or apart from the body I do not know, God knows– was caught up into Paradise and heard inexpressible words, which a man is not permitted to speak. On behalf of such a man I will boast; but on my own behalf I will not boast, except in regard to my weaknesses. For if I do wish to boast I will not be foolish, for I will be speaking the truth; but I refrain from this, so that no one will credit me with more than he sees in me or hears from me.

2 Corinthians 12:1-6 NASB

(This Man is Christ Jesus that Paul speaks of. We are to boast only of Christ not of ourselves for we do not understand such heavenly things.)

(Because we do not know such things, we should be careful not to speak on matters pertaining to such, as others might perceive us as knowing as God knows which we do not only Christ does.)

Because of the surpassing greatness of the revelations, for this reason, to keep me from exalting myself, there was given me a thorn in the flesh, a messenger of Satan to torment me—to keep me from exalting myself!

(Many people call this a conscience or voice; it is not of God that these things come to mind but by Satan that we are tempted to think on such things as to appear more important than others.)

Concerning this I implored the Lord three times that it might leave me. And He has said to me, "My grace is sufficient for you, for power is perfected in weakness." Most gladly, therefore, I will rather boast about my weaknesses, so that the power of Christ may dwell in me. Therefore, I am well content with weaknesses, with insults, with distresses, with persecutions, with difficulties, for Christ's sake; for when I am weak, then I am strong.

2 Corinthians 12:7-10 NASB

Praise the Lord for your failures and shortcomings for in these things God's Grace through Christ Jesus becomes the Power of Christ in you when you are weak.)

ALIVE IN CHRIST DEAD TO SELF:

We know that we have passed out of death into life because we love the brethren. He who does not love abides in death.
1 John 3:14 NASB

(Apostle Paul says "to live is Christ. To die is gain."

We do not live unless Christ lives in us. We become circumcised/ cut off from the flesh when we choose this Crucified life.)

Who are your brethren?

Definition:
Brethren: Plural of Brother: a male who has the same parents as another or one parent in common with another

2: one related to another by common ties or interests

3: a fellow member –used as a title for ministers in some evangelical denominations

4: one of a type similar to another

(Are we not created in the same way as all who are flesh and bone?)

Having this in common makes us all brethren of flesh, now even more so those in Christ, brethren of Spirit.)

(And Jesus says this on how we are to love, and it is only by living in the Spirit can such a love be given as we are not capable of such love without the Spirit.)

But I say to you that everyone who is angry with his brother shall be guilty before the court; and whoever says to his brother, 'You good-for-nothing,' shall be guilty before the supreme court; and whoever says, 'You fool,' shall be guilty enough to go into the fiery hell.

Matthew 5:22 NASB

FRUITS:

Manifestations are things of the flesh

Fruit of the spirit is not of the flesh but of the Spirit.

Man does not control the spirit the spirit takes over the man, just as one can be possessed by evil Spirits we choose to be filled with the Holy Spirit and this is the Spirit walking not us and being, so we are crucified of flesh and alive in Spirit.

The Spirit now is Manifest in you and He intercedes in all aspects of life.

The Spirit walks/ you walk
The Spirit breathes/ you breathe
The Spirit produces fruit/your bear that fruit

Nothing you do, is of the Spirit
Everything is now done through you from the Spirit.

This is called the crucified life
It is the Spirits fruit never ours.
A branch cannot bear its own fruit separate from the tree

As such the tree supplies the branch with the fruits it is to yield fruit according to the roots.

If one is rooted in self or anything other than God, the tree is not of the Spirit and the branches will have no fruit to bear.

Do not be surprised, brethren, if the world hates you. We know that we have passed out of death into life because we love the brethren. He who does not love abides in death. Everyone who hates his brother is a murderer; and you know that no murderer has eternal life abiding in him. We know love by this, that He laid down His life for us; and we ought to lay down our lives for the brethren. But whoever has the world's goods, and sees his brother in need and closes his heart against him, how does the love of God abide in him? Little children, let us not love with word or with tongue, but indeed and truth. We will know by this that we are of the truth and will assure our heart before Him in whatever our heart condemns us; for God is greater than our heart and knows all things. Beloved, if our heart does not condemn us, we have confidence before God; and whatever we ask we receive from Him, because we keep His commandments and do the things that are pleasing in His sight. This is His commandment, that we believe in the name of His Son Jesus Christ, and love one another, just as He commanded us. The one who keeps His commandments abides in Him, and He in him. We know by this that He abides in us, by the Spirit whom He has given us.

1 John 3:13-24 NASB

CHERISH DISCIPLINE:

(In this world we live in there is a massive audience, a world theater full of lost and confused, anxious and afraid, searching for hope and truth by any means necessary. Those in Christ born again in the Spirit must not give into offering hope as the world does but to let the Power of The Holy Spirit work through us and stay steadfast in the Truth of Christ as we are called to do.)

Now may the God of hope fill you with all joy and peace in believing, so that you will abound in hope by the power of the Holy Spirit.
Romans 15:13 NASB

Therefore, since we have so great a cloud of witnesses surrounding us, let us also lay aside every encumbrance and the sin which so easily entangles us, and let us run with endurance the race that is set before us, fixing our eyes on Jesus, the author and perfecter of faith, who for the joy set before Him endured the cross, despising the shame, and has sat down at the right hand of the throne of God.

(We have not suffered as our brothers in Christ before us. Our suffering is one of principalities do not flesh and blood as theirs, so let us keep endurance and stand strong for it is easier for us now, As we have the help of The Holy Spirit to make a path in the way we should walk, and we are to walk according to the fruit of the Spirit and live according to these same first fruits.)

But the fruit of the Spirit is love, joy, peace, patience, kindness, goodness, faithfulness, gentleness, self-control; against such things there is no law. Now those who belong to Christ Jesus have crucified the flesh with its passions and desires. If we live by the Spirit, let us also walk by the Spirit. Let us not become boastful, challenging one another, envying one another.
Galatians 5:22

For consider Him who has endured such hostility by sinners against Himself, so that you will not grow weary and lose heart. You have not yet resisted to the point of shedding blood in your striving against sin; and you have forgotten the exhortation, which is addressed to you as sons,

(Embrace and welcome with full and open hearts the discipline that comes from our Father for by it we are refined in Righteousness in Christ. Forged by fire of the Holy Spirit made to stand against any and all types of evil without growing weary or faint.)

I advise you to buy from Me gold refined by fire so that you may become rich, and white garments so that you may clothe yourself, and that the shame of your nakedness will not be revealed; and eye salve to anoint your eyes so that you may see. Those whom I love, I reprove and discipline; therefore, be zealous and repent.
Revelation 3:18

(Invest in the Wisdom of God our Father by loving to be disciplined
And in constant study of the Word and received in us by the Holy Spirit. So that you may see and hear without confusion.)

"My son, do not regard lightly the discipline of the Lord, Nor faint when you are reproved by Him; For those whom the Lord loves

He disciplines, And He scourges every son whom He receives." It is for discipline that you endure; God deals with you as with sons; for what son is there whom his father does not discipline? But if you are without discipline, of which all have become partakers, then you are illegitimate children and not sons.

Furthermore, we had earthly fathers to discipline us, and we respected them; shall we not much rather be subject to the Father of spirits, and live? For they disciplined us for a short time as seemed best to them, but He disciplines us for our good, so that we may share His holiness.

(It may at times seem like some are getting the short end of the stick, those in Christ will be put through the fire of Our Father's kiln so that we may bear the peaceful fruits of righteousness in Christ.)

All discipline for the moment seems not to be joyful, but sorrowful; yet to those who have been trained by it, afterwards it yields the peaceful fruit of righteousness. Therefore, strengthen the hands that are weak and the knees that are feeble, and make straight paths for your feet, so that the limb which is lame may not be put out of joint, but rather be healed. Pursue peace with all men, and the sanctification without which no one will see the Lord. See to it that no one comes short of the grace of God.
Hebrews 12:1

Beloved, do not be surprised at the fiery ordeal among you, which comes upon you for your testing, as though some strange thing were happening to you; but to the degree that you share the sufferings of Christ, keep on rejoicing, so that also at the revelation of His glory you may rejoice with exultation. If you are reviled for the name of Christ, you are blessed, because the Spirit of glory and of God rests on you.
1 Peter 4:12

(Those in Christ are center stage in a world who seeks the Truth that can only be found in our Lord and Savior Jesus Christ, let us be of one accord and let them see the light of Christ shine through us so that they too will come to the Salvation and receive a Peace that surpasses all understanding.)

OF CHRIST NOT OF SELF:

Now you are Christ's body, and individually members of it. And God has appointed in the church
(Not a building but those in Christ)

first apostles, second prophets, third teachers, then miracles, then gifts of healings, helps, administrations, various kinds of tongues.

All are not apostles, are they?
All are not prophets, are they?
All are not teachers, are they?
All are not workers of miracles, are they?
All do not have gifts of healings, do they?
All do not speak with tongues, do they?
All do not interpret, do they?

But earnestly desire the greater gifts. (Do not be envious of the Spirits gifts in others but earnestly desire the greater gifts that are not seen) And I show you a still more excellent way.

1 Corinthians 12:27-31 NASB

If I speak with the tongues of men and of angels, but do not have love, I have become a noisy gong or a clanging cymbal.

If I have the gift of prophecy and know all mysteries and all knowledge; and if I have all faith, so as to remove mountains, but do not have love, I am nothing.

And if I give all my possessions to feed the poor, and if I surrender my body to be burned, but do not have love, it profits me nothing.

Love is patient, love is kind and is not jealous; love does not brag and is not arrogant, does not act unbecomingly; it does not seek its own, is not provoked, does not take into account a wrong suffered, does not rejoice in unrighteousness, but rejoices with the truth; bears all things, believes all things, hopes all things, endures all things. Love never fails; but if there are gifts of prophecy, they will be done away; if there are tongues, they will cease; if there is knowledge, it will be done away. For we know in part, and we prophesy in part; but when the perfect comes, the partial will be done away.

When I was a child, I used to speak like a child, think like a child, reason like a child; when I became a man, I did away with childish things. For now, we see in a mirror dimly, but then face to face; now I know in part, but then I will know fully just as I also have been fully known.

But now faith, hope, love, abide these three; but the greatest of these is

LOVE

1 Corinthians 13:1-13 NASB

We love because He first loved us.
(Not by ourselves, but because of Christ we love

If someone says, "I love God," and hates his brother, he is a liar; for the one who does not love his brother whom he has seen, cannot love God whom he has not seen. And this commandment we have from Him, that the one who loves God should love his brother also.

1 John 4:19-21 NASB

DISCONNECTING FROM THE FLESH:

(More and more as I spend every moment, I am awake talking with God and growing closer to Him I find less of myself in me and more of Christ, not that I feel more important than anyone else or better than anyone but rather at perfect peace in not being me. The things in the world around me are all sorts of chaos and nothing good and at times extremely difficult to understand. I do not miss how I once was and have much sorrow for others that continue to want to live that way.)

(At times, a deep inner mourning for those I have never met which words cannot express.)

(I wish to only have conversations about the Love others have received in Christ and hear how He is working in their lives and share stories of our Fathers Amazing Grace and Mercy towards us and how we are growing in Him. All other news in the world is bland, boring, and troublesome and gives me a bitter stomach when swallowed. Knowledge of the world used to taste good and now I find it repulsive and disgusting.)

(This new creation that I yearned for deep within my heart and called out to God for has come with unexplainable Peace and Joy which words cannot express and with it much sorrow that surpasses understanding.)

(My only hope and prayers are for The Fathers Will to be done through me so that others will see Him fully in all His Glory and turn from their prideful ways and chasing after all that is offered by men in a world which will come to ruin when Our Lord returns.)

But as for you, speak the things which are fitting for sound doctrine. Older men are to be temperate, dignified, sensible, sound in faith, in love, in perseverance. Older women likewise are to be reverent in their behavior, not malicious gossips nor enslaved to much wine, teaching what is good, so that they may encourage the young women to love their husbands, to love their children, to be sensible, pure, workers at home, kind, being subject to their own husbands, so that the word of God will not be dishonored. Likewise urge the young men to be sensible; in all things show yourself to be an example of good deeds, with purity in doctrine, dignified, sound in speech, which is beyond reproach, so that the opponent will be put to shame, having nothing bad to say about us. Urge bond slaves to be subject to their own masters in everything, to be well-pleasing, not argumentative, not pilfering, but showing all good faith so that they will adorn the doctrine of God our Savior in every respect. For the grace of God has appeared, bringing salvation to all men, instructing us to deny ungodliness and worldly desires and to live sensibly, righteously, and godly in the present age, looking for the blessed hope and the appearing of the glory of our great God and Savior, Christ Jesus, who gave Himself for us to redeem us from every lawless deed, and to purify for Himself a people for His own possession, zealous for good deeds. These things speak and exhort and reprove with all authority. Let no one disregard you. Titus 2:1-15 NASB

Remind them to be subject to rulers, to authorities, to be obedient, to be ready for every good deed, to malign no one, to be peaceable, gentle, showing every consideration for all men.

For we also once were foolish ourselves, disobedient, deceived, enslaved to various lusts and pleasures, spending our life in malice and envy, hateful, hating one another. But when the kindness of God our Savior and His love for mankind appeared, He saved us, not on the basis of deeds which we have done in righteousness, but according to His mercy, by the washing of regeneration and renewing by the Holy Spirit, whom He poured out upon us richly through Jesus Christ our Savior, so that being justified by His grace we would be made heirs according to the hope of eternal life. This is a trustworthy statement; and concerning these things I want you to speak confidently, so that those who have believed God will be careful to engage in good deeds. These things are good and profitable for men. But avoid foolish controversies and genealogies and strife and disputes about the Law, for they are unprofitable and worthless. Reject a factious man after a first and second warning, knowing that such a man is perverted and is sinning, being self-condemned.

Titus 3:1-11 NASB

CONFORMITY IS AN OPEN DOOR TO DECEPTION:

(Take care not to mix the views of the world with the Truth of the Spirit this is a slippery slope and if in the Spirit should cause instant conviction within.) (Although we are in the world and not yet complete for that comes when He Returns, we are not to be of the world.)

And do not be conformed to this world, but be transformed by the renewing of your mind, so that you may prove what the will of God is, that which is good, acceptable, and perfect. Romans 12:2

But the fruit of the Spirit is love, joy, peace, patience, kindness, goodness, faithfulness, gentleness, self-control; against such things there is no law. Now those who belong to Christ Jesus have crucified the flesh with its passions and desires. If we live by the Spirit, let us also walk by the Spirit. Let us not become boastful, challenging one another, envying one another.

Galatians 5:22-26

(The Spirit has put on my heart convicted me to not let in with my eyes the daily talk and conspiracy of the world's views on what is happening. I do not need to know WHAT because by the Spirit in me through Christ Jesus I know WHY.

(Conspiracy:) the revealing of a divine truth
(Visible to the eye of the flesh)
(Should be of no concern to those in Christ and walking in the Spirit.

(Prophecy:) Gods Will be done in all things not seen and is the Word by which all things that were made were made from that which is not seen in the beginning.

(Invisible to the eyes of the flesh and only understood by the Spirit and received by the Spirit of
Those in Christ) (Born Again) (rebirth from flesh to Spirit)

The worries of the world should not be burdensome to those in Christ as our Peace comes from understanding by the Spirit that all that happens is of God's will and not understood by those outside of the Spirit.

RECONCILIATION:

Therefore, having been justified by faith, we have peace with God through our Lord Jesus Christ, through whom also we have obtained our introduction by faith into this grace in which we stand; and we exult in hope of the glory of God. And not only this, but we also exult in our tribulations, knowing that tribulation brings about perseverance; and perseverance, proven character; and proven character, hope; and hope does not disappoint, because the love of God has been poured out within our hearts through the Holy Spirit who was given to us.

(When you accept and believe that Jesus is the Son of God, and He was sent to pay for the debt of sin that we all from the beginning were accursed with and to introduce us to The Father as being justified by Faith we are now given Peace with God our Father and are adopted into God's family as we because of sin were orphans and could not see God. Now with this adoption comes the gift of the Holy Spirit who fills us with the love of God and a peace which surpasses all understanding.)

(By God's Grace we have been saved through faith in Christ Jesus so that we may be called Sons of God and no longer condemned to death by sin but given a new life in Him. Made complete by Christ there is no other way.

For while we were still helpless, at the right time Christ died for the ungodly. (All of humanity)

For one will hardly die for a righteous man, though perhaps for the good man someone would dare even to die.

(Do you know anyone in the world we live in that would give everything including their life for someone who is righteous in their own eyes)

But God demonstrates His own love toward us, in that while we were yet sinners, Christ died for us. Much more than, having now been justified by His blood, we shall be saved from the wrath of God through Him.

(Not by anything we can do but because Jesus Christ conquered death and was Resurrected in the Flesh and Spirit and by this the ultimate act of Love we have Life in Him and He in us. A new creation)

For if while we were enemies we were reconciled to God through the death of His Son, much more, having been reconciled, we shall be saved by His life. And not only this, but we also exult in God through our Lord Jesus Christ, through whom we have now received the reconciliation. Romans 5:1-11 NASB

THANKSGIVING:

Father we give you thanks not as the world gives you thanks but we thank you for what we are not

And we do this because through the Grace of your love for us and in Christ Jesus we are in the Spirit what we are not in the flesh.

And we thank you

For all things that are graciously received today and every day we give you the glory, honor, and praise.

Shout joyfully to the Lord, all the earth.
Serve the Lord with gladness; Come before Him with joyful singing.
Know that the Lord Himself is God; It is He who has made us, and not we ourselves; We are His people and the sheep of His pasture.

Enter His gates with thanksgiving And His courts with praise.

Give thanks to Him, bless His name.
For the Lord is good; His lovingkindness is everlasting And His faithfulness to all generations.
Psalms 100:1-5 NASB

STRONG AND UNASHAMED:

Suffer hardship with me, as a good soldier of Christ Jesus. No soldier in active service entangles himself in the affairs of everyday life, so that he may please the one who enlisted him as a soldier.

(What do you spend your day talking about and what kinds of things are you entertaining in your life? Are you concerned with the same things the world is? What feelings and thoughts arise from such chatter?)

Also, if anyone competes as an athlete, he does not win the prize unless he competes according to the rules. The hard-working farmer ought to be the first to receive his share of the crops.

Consider what I say, for the Lord will give you understanding in everything. It is a trustworthy statement: For if we died with Him, we will also live with Him; If we endure, we will also reign with Him; If we deny Him, He also will deny us; If we are faithless, He remains faithful, for He cannot deny Himself.

(Are you living your life by the Spirit or becoming just as the rest of the world conformed to the gossip and worrisome chatter of what will come and go just as all things have come and gone? Do you give your time and attention to that which will pass away and do your thoughts, feelings and actions bring Glory to God?

Be strong in Faith by the Spirit and let His truth be your truth in every response, coming from the

Spirit and moved into action by Faith in knowing that all things done by the Spirit are

Righteousness in Christ Jesus and will be pleasing God the Father and will be soft and pleasant to the ears of those who hear.)

Remind them of these things, and solemnly charge them in the presence of God not to wrangle about words, which is useless and leads to the ruin of the hearers.
Be diligent to present yourself approved to God as a workman who does not need to be ashamed, accurately handling the word of truth. But avoid worldly and empty chatter, for it will lead to further ungodliness, Nevertheless, the firm foundation of God stands, having this seal,

"The Lord knows those who are His," and, "Everyone who names the name of the Lord is to abstain from wickedness."

(If you speak in the name of the Lord let it not be from the lips of the flesh and come from the mind of a man all things must be from the Spirit, guided and filtered through the Spirit, for the tongue of a man is wicked and full of self. It is not we who do Righteous things but the Spirit
Proceeds in advance to open the door for His works not ours.
And by this we should be SLOW

TO SPEAK, QUICK TO LISTEN, SLOW TO ANGER.)

(Anyone who is quick to anger will be quick to speak in that anger and will not hear the Spirit
Speak and is not in the Spirit But is self-serving of the flesh.)

Now in a large house there are not only gold and silver vessels, but also vessels of wood and of earthenware, and some to honor and some to dishonor. Therefore, if anyone cleanses himself from these things, he will be a vessel for honor, sanctified, useful to the Master, prepared for every good work.

(Do you have any prize possessions? Car/ house/ money/ job/ pets / church congregation silver collection/ things of value to you?

(Ask yourself, of these things which are honorable to God, and which are not.
Are you grateful for these things that are honorable, or do you boast about them and place them higher than your relationship with God?)

Now flee from youthful lusts and pursue righteousness, faith, love, and peace, with those who call on the Lord from a pure heart. But refuse foolish and ignorant speculations, knowing that they produce quarrels.

(We in Christ should not be involved in such things as all others
HOT TOPICS = HOT GOSSIP
and should be avoided for it will lead to a self-serving mind not of the Spirit. do not entertain
such things as they will cause you to fall into sin.)

The Lord's bondservant must not be quarrelsome, but be kind to all, able to teach, patient when wronged, with gentleness correcting those who are in opposition, if perhaps God may grant them repentance leading to the knowledge of the truth, and they may come to their senses and escape from the snare of the devil, having been held captive by him to do his will. 2 Timothy 2:3-7, 11-16, 19-26 NASB

(We in Christ are ambassadors of The Gospel of Truth by the Spirit and are the lamp that contains the Light which shines as He is the Light that all the world sees in us

Keep the glass on your lamp clean from the filth of the world (Your eyes)

Keep your lamp full of oil
(This is accomplished by receiving the Word of God from the Holy Spirit through Scripture it is not merely reading it is Listening The Word of God is Spoken to the Spirit and received by the Spirit in us.
(He who has an ear let him (HEAR) what the Spirit says.)

(Be ready and available at all times in the Spirit so that the Lord may work through you for the Glory of God)

(Be present and in the world (not of the world) so that the light of Christ who is the life of man may be seen in you as ambassadors to the Gospel and all who see it be enamored and drawn to Christ for Salvation. (Being careful not to boast of self but to boast only of our Lord and

Savior Christ Jesus

And that We do all things for the Glory of God the Father of all creation of the heavens and earth.)

ORPHANS AND WIDOWS:

But one who looks intently at the perfect law, the law of liberty, and abides by it, not having become a forgetful hearer but an effectual doer, this man will be blessed in what he does.

(Having received the Word of God
And being liberated from sin by Christ we must not forget what we have received in teaching by the Spirit and apply it in all aspects of our lives not just by hearing the Word but by doing.)

If anyone thinks himself to be religious, and yet does not bridle his tongue but deceives his own heart, this man's religion is worthless.

(What comes from our lips must be From the Spirit not our mind for our mind is quick to speak of things pertaining to the flesh and results in self-proclaimed righteousness of which we have none outside of Christ.)

Pure and undefiled religion in the sight of our God and Father is this: to visit orphans and widows in their distress, and to keep oneself unstained by the world. James 1:25-27 NASB

(If received by the Spirit the definition of orphans and widows would be defined by the Spirit.)

(Visit with unbelievers when they are struggling and suffering and in love of the Spirit comfort them

Be in the world and guide the world to Christ. Do not give Band-Aids as the world gives but offer them the love and Peace through Christ Jesus who heals all wounds of the Soul and body.)

(Orphans= those having not accepted Christ and are not born of the Spirit and still living in the flesh.)

(Widows= A man or a woman born again in Christ who has a Spouse who has not received
Christ.)

The one in Christ is Alive
The one without is still dead (not born again) in Christ.

WINNING WHEN LOSING:

Beware of the dogs, beware of the evil workers, beware of the false circumcision; for we are the true circumcision, who worship in the Spirit of God and glory in Christ Jesus and put no confidence in the flesh,

(World's definition of Circumcision
Rely on and put confidence in the things that make you feel good and take pride in them.)
(Worship of self and Pridefulness)

(Spiritual Circumcision definition to cut off all confidence in your own mind and self-pride and rely only on Christ.)
(Worship of Spirit and Pride in Christ not in self)

But whatever things were gain to me, those things I have counted as loss for the sake of Christ.
More than that, I count all things to be loss in view of the surpassing value of knowing Christ Jesus my Lord, for whom I have suffered the loss of all things, and count them but rubbish so that I may gain Christ, and may be found in Him,

(There is no value in anything that has no life eternally.
We place value on things that rust and crumble and we even place value in relationships that pull us away from our relationship with God in Christ Jesus, and also, we put value in sermons and pastors which do not drive us to a deeper growth in Christ.

What do you put value in that the Spirit is convicting you to lose in your life?

To live is Christ to die is gain

(Not in the physical sense but when living in Christ, the loss of all that has no value being dead becomes gain.)

not having a righteousness of my own derived from the Law, but that which is through faith in Christ, the righteousness which comes from God on the basis of faith, that I may know Him and the power of His resurrection and the fellowship of His sufferings, being conformed to His death; in order that I may attain to the resurrection from the dead. Not that I have already obtained it or have already become perfect, but I press on so that I may lay hold of that for which also I was laid hold of by Christ Jesus. Brethren, I do not regard myself as having laid hold of it yet.

but one thing I do: forgetting what lies behind and reaching forward to what lies ahead, I press on toward the goal for the prize of the upward call of God in Christ Jesus.

Let us therefore, as many as are perfect, have this attitude; and if in anything you have a different attitude, God will reveal that also to you; however, let us keep living by that same standard to which we have attained. Brethren, join in following my example, and observe those who walk according to the pattern you have in us.

For many walk, of whom I often told you, and now tell you even weeping, that they are enemies of the cross of Christ, whose end is destruction, whose god is their appetite, and whose glory is in their shame, who set their minds on earthly things.

(We are not to take pleasure or pride in the things of the world as the world does for all things are subject to God and all things not of God will go to destruction.)

(Put no value or place any confidence in anything of the flesh or its desires of the mind
But in Christ is all Faith and assuredness.)

For our citizenship is in heaven, from which also we eagerly wait for a Savior, the Lord Jesus Christ, who will transform the body of our humble state into conformity with the body of His glory, by the exertion of the power that He has even to subject all things to Himself.

Philippians 3:2-3, 7-21 NASB

SPIRITUAL WISDOM:

PRO VERB S

PRO
(Earlier than: prior to before)

VERB
(Action word)

S
(Spirit)

(For those in Christ the Holy Spirit should always come before anything you choose whether it be a thought feeling or response or action.)

To know wisdom and instruction, To discern the sayings of understanding, To receive instruction in wise behavior, Righteousness, justice, and equity; To give prudence to the naive, To the youth knowledge and discretion, A wise man will hear and increase in learning, And a man of understanding will acquire wise counsel, To understand a proverb and a figure, The words of the wise and their riddles. The fear of the Lord is the beginning of knowledge; Fools despise wisdom and instruction.
Proverbs 1:2

(We receive Wisdom and Knowledge from the Holy Spirit by the Word and then apply it in our works by Faith and to ignore the Holy Spirit is to deny Christ and all Wisdom and teaching of the Father.) (disobedience)

(The Holy Spirit speaks consistently, and you must always be listening to her; she will keep you from harm.)

(Ever wonder why your life is in shambles and you feel like nothing ever goes right in your situation?

(Are you listening to the Spirit or talking over her?)

(There is no one to blame but ourselves. When we do not listen, we make un-informed costly decisions that are not wise in God's eyes.)

Wisdom shouts in the street, She lifts her voice in the square; At the head of the noisy streets, she cries out; At the entrance of the gates in the city she utters her sayings: "How long, O naive ones, will you love being simple-minded? And scoffers delight themselves in scoffing and fools hate knowledge? Turn to my reproof, Behold, I will pour out my spirit on you; I will make my words known to you.

(We do not read Scripture and Comprehend the Spiritual meaning of it. The Word is received in us by the Spirit. We have no wisdom of Spiritual things with our own eyes, but the Spirit reveals all Wisdom from The Father.)

Because I called and you refused, I stretched out my hand and no one paid attention; And you neglected all my counsel And did not want my reproof; I will also laugh at your calamity; I will mock when your dread comes, When your dread comes like a storm And your calamity comes like a whirlwind, When

distress and anguish come upon you. Then they will call on me, but I will not answer; They will seek me diligently, but they will not find me, because they hated knowledge and did not choose the fear of the Lord. They would not accept my counsel; they spurned all my reproof. So, they shall eat of the fruit of their own way and be satiated with their own devices. For the way-wardness of the naive will kill them, And the complacency of fools will destroy them. But he who (LISTENS) to me shall live securely and will be at ease from the dread of evil."
Proverbs 1:20

(Peace from all worries and evil things comes from Spiritual understanding, Spiritual understanding comes from Wisdom, Wisdom is from God, received by the Spirit of those in Christ who LISTEN to the Holy Spirit and heed to Her teachings.)

(Accept Christ as your Personal Savior and the Son of God), (being Born Again, a new creation, one in the Spirit of Christ, having now put away the desires of the flesh.
And receive the gift of the Holy Spirit who will be the rudder of your ship and guide you and keep you on Course for the Will of The Father to work through you in all things.)

My son, if you will receive my words And treasure my commandments within you, Make your ear attentive to wisdom, Incline your heart to understanding; For if you cry for discernment, Lift your voice for understanding; If you seek her as silver And search for her as for hidden treasures; Then you will discern the fear of the Lord And discover the knowledge of God. For the Lord gives wisdom; From His mouth comes knowledge and understanding. He stores up sound wisdom for the upright; He is a shield to those who walk in integrity, Guarding the paths of justice, And He preserves the way of His godly ones. Then you will discern righteousness and justice and equity and every good course.

(Receive the Holy Spirit's teaching, Live by the Spirit, walk by the Spirit, do nothing of your own accord and worldly knowledge. But in all things seek the Lord and He will make your paths straight.)

For wisdom will enter your heart And
knowledge will be pleasant to your soul.
Discretion will guard you; Understanding will watch over you,

(Invisible Holy Spirit Protection)

To deliver you from the way of evil, From the man who speaks perverse things; From those who leave the paths of uprightness To walk in the ways of darkness; Who delight in doing evil And rejoice in the perversity of evil; Whose paths are crooked, And who are devious in their ways; To deliver you from the strange woman, From the adulteress who flatters with her words; That leaves the companion of her youth And forgets the covenant of her God; For her house sinks down to death And her tracks lead to the dead; None who go to her return again, Nor do they reach the paths of life.

So, you will walk in the way of good men and keep to the paths of the righteous. For the upright will live in the land and the blameless will remain in it.

(THE WAY OF THE LORD)
OR
(THE WAY OF DEATH)
But the wicked will be cut off from the land and

TEMPERAMENT:

(As we go through our day from the moment we open our eyes, track your thoughts during the day and be in conversation with the Spirit about them.)

PROVERBS
(PRO)(VERB)(S)

PRO= BEFORE
VERB= ACTION WORD
S= Spirit

(Let the Holy Spirit proceed
(Come before you) in your thoughts, feelings, and responses in every situation.)

The plans of the heart belong to man, But the answer of the tongue is from the Lord.
All the ways of a man are clean in his own sight, But the Lord weighs the motives.
Commit your works to the Lord And your plans will be established.
The Lord has made everything for its own purpose, Even the wicked for the day of evil. Everyone who is proud in heart is an abomination to the Lord; Assuredly, he will not be unpunished.
By lovingkindness and truth iniquity is atoned for, and by the fear of the Lord one keeps away from evil.

When a man's ways are pleasing to the Lord, He makes even his enemies to be at peace with him.
Better is a little with righteousness Than great income with injustice.
The mind of man plans his way, But the Lord directs his steps.
A divine decision is in the lips of the king; His mouth should not err in judgment.
A just balance and scales belong to the Lord; All the weights of the bag are His concern.
It is an abomination for kings to commit wicked acts, for a throne is established on righteousness.
Righteous lips are the delight of kings, and he who speaks right is loved.
The fury of a king is like messengers of death, but a wise man will appease it.
In the light of a king's face is life, and his favor is like a cloud with the spring rain.
How much better it is to get wisdom than gold! And to get understanding is to be chosen above silver.
The highway of the upright is to depart from evil; He who watches his way preserves his life.
Pride goes before destruction, and a haughty spirit before stumbling.
It is better to be humble in spirit with the lowly Than to divide the spoil with the proud.
He who gives attention to the word will find good and blessed is he who trusts in the Lord.
The wise in heart will be called understanding, and sweetness of speech increases persuasiveness.
Understanding is a fountain of life to one who has it, But the discipline of fools is folly.
The heart of the wise instructs his mouth and adds persuasiveness to his lips. Pleasant words are a honeycomb, Sweet to the soul and healing to the bones.

There is a way which seems right to a man, but its end is the way of death.
A worker's appetite works for him, for his hunger urges him on.
A worthless man digs up evil, while his words are like scorching fire.
A perverse man spreads strife, and a slanderer separates intimate friends.
A man of violence entices his neighbor and leads him in a way that is not good.
He who winks his eyes does so to devise perverse things; He who compresses his lips brings evil to pass.
A gray head is a crown of glory; It is found in the way of righteousness.
He who is slow to anger is better than the mighty, and he who rules his spirit, than he who captures a city.
The lot is cast into the lap, but its every decision is from the Lord.
Proverbs 16:1

WORTHY OF GODS LOVE AND GRACE IN CHRIST:

(You are more than enough in Christ.)

(In Christ you are given life not as the world gives but by the Grace of our Heavenly Father the Alpha and Omega The God of all creation of all the heavens and earth.)

Therefore, having been justified by faith, we have peace with God through our Lord Jesus Christ, through whom also we have obtained our introduction by faith into this grace in which we stand; and we exult in hope of the glory of God. And not only this, but we also exult in our tribulations, knowing that tribulation brings about perseverance; and perseverance, proven character; and proven character, hope; and hope does not disappoint, because the love of God has been poured out within our hearts through the Holy Spirit who was given to us.
Romans 5:1

REPROOF AND HEALING:

Brethren, even if anyone is caught in any trespass, you who are spiritual, restore such a one in a spirit of gentleness; each one looking to yourself, so that you too will not be tempted.

(Letting the Holy Spirit proceed before you in matters of correction among believers so as to not become righteous of self so that the healing is one of the same in Christ Jesus.)

Bear one another's burdens, and thereby fulfill the law of Christ. For if anyone thinks he is something when he is nothing, he deceives himself. But each one must examine his own work, and then he will have reason for boasting in regard to himself alone, and not in regard to another.

(It is easy for those in Christ to be deceived into displaying outwardly a showing of our Faith in Christ and being seen by others as Prideful
(a holier than thou perception)

(Take pride in your Faith in Christ from within and by doing so you will be seen as humble among those who do not believe.)

For each one will bear his own load. The one who is taught the word is to share all good things with the one who teaches him. Do not be deceived,

(As those in Christ are taught by the Holy Spirit share all the good things that you have been able to put into practice with others in Christ and in prayer give thanks and praise to the Father for such things.)

God is not mocked; for whatever a man sows, this he will also reap. For the one who sows to his own flesh will from the flesh reap corruption, but the one who sows to the Spirit will from the Spirit reap eternal life.

(All good things come from Our Father so let us do all things through Christ according to His Word and given to us by the Holy Spirit and the blessings will be a reward not for us but to those who receive Christ through us.)

Let us not lose heart in doing good, for in due time we will reap if we do not grow weary. So then, while we have opportunity, let us do good to all people, and especially to those who are of the household of the faith.
Galatians 6:1

THE MEETING OF OUR SAVIOR:

(Those in Christ who have passed will be resurrected and taken up and those in Christ that are still alive at the time of the return of Jesus will be taken up to meet Him and those that had died in the Air together.)
(Those in Christ born again, a new creation, one of Spirit, no longer satisfying the desires of the flesh and living by the fruit of the Spirit they will be spared from the Tribulation that is to come upon the rest of the world that turned their back on the Wisdom of God's Word and did not believe that Jesus is the Son of God and the Savior of all Sins.)

"Now at that time Michael, the great prince who stands guard over the sons of your people, will arise. And there will be a time of distress such as never occurred since there was a nation until that time; and at that time your people, everyone who is found written in the book, will be rescued. Many of those who sleep in the dust of the ground will awake, these to everlasting life, but the others to disgrace and everlasting contempt. Those who have insight will shine brightly like the brightness of the expanse of heaven, and those who lead the many to righteousness, like the stars forever and ever.
Daniel 12:1

In My Father's house are many dwelling places; if it were not so, I would have told you; for I go to prepare a place for you. If I

go and prepare a place for you, I will come again and receive you to Myself, that where I am, there you may be also.
John 14:2

Because you have kept the word of My perseverance, I also will keep you from the hour of testing, that hour, which is about to come upon the entire world, to test those who dwell on the earth. I am coming quickly; hold fast what you have, so that no one will take your crown.
Revelation 3:10

For the Lord Himself will descend from heaven with a shout, with the voice of the archangel and with the trumpet of God, and the dead in Christ will rise first. Then we who are alive and remain will be caught up together with them in the clouds to meet the Lord in the air, and so we shall always be with the Lord. Therefore comfort one another with these words.
1 Thessalonians 4:16

I tell you, on that night there will be two in one bed; one will be taken and the other will be left. There will be two women grinding at the same place; one will be taken and the other will be left. [Two men will be in the field; one will be taken and the other will be left."]
Luke 17:34

SABBATH AND CIVIL YEARS:

THE JEWISH CALENDAR

The Jews used two kinds of calendars:
Civil Calendar—official calendar of kings, childbirth, and contracts.
Sacred Calendar—from which festivals were computed.

NAMES OF MONTHS	CORRESPONDS WITH	NO. OF DAYS	MONTH OF CIVIL YEAR	MONTH OF SACRED YEAR
TISHRI	Sept.-Oct.	30 days	1st	7th
HESHVAN	Oct.-Nov.	29 or 30	2nd	8th
CHISLEV	Nov.-Dec.	29 or 30	3rd	9th
TEBETH	Dec.-Jan.	29	4th	10th
SHEBAT	Jan.-Feb.	30	5th	11th
ADAR	Feb.-Mar.	29 or 30	6th	12th
NISAN	Mar.-Apr.	30	7th	1st
IYAR	Apr.-May	29	8th	2nd
SIVAN	May-June	30	9th	3rd
TAMMUZ	June-July	29	10th	4th
AB	July-Aug.	30	11th	5th
*ELUL	Aug.-Sept.	29	12th	6th

The Jewish day was from sunset to sunset, in 8 equal parts:

FIRST WATCH.........SUNSET TO 9 P.M.
SECOND WATCH.......9 P.M. TO MIDNIGHT
THIRD WATCH..........MIDNIGHT TO 3 A.M.
FOURTH WATCH.......3 A.M. TO SUNRISE

FIRST WATCH.........SUNRISE TO 9 A.M.
SECOND WATCH.......9 A.M. TO NOON
THIRD WATCH.........NOON TO 3 P.M.
FOURTH WATCH.......3 P.M. TO SUNSET

*Hebrew months were alternately 30 and 29 days long. Their year, shorter than ours, had 354 days. Therefore, about every 3 years (7 times in 19 years) an extra 29-day-month, VEADAR, was added between ADAR and NISAN.

This is a chart of civil/sacred years starting 27/28 AD. The Civil year is indicated in parentheses followed by the next seven Sacred/sabbath years

I put • next to the year we are entering into the 6th sacred/ sabbath year.

I started them in 1693 AD for easier reference.

(1693)

1694	1700	1707	1714	1721	1728	1735

(1742)

1743	1749	1756	1763	1770	1777	1784

(1791)

1792	1798	1805	1812	1819	1826	1833

(1840)

1841	1847	1854	1861	1868	1875	1882

(1889)

1890	1896	1903	1910	1917	1924	1931

(1938)

1939	1945	1952	1959	1966	1973	1980

(1987)

1988	1994	2001	2008	2015	•2022•	2029

(2036)

2037	2043	2050	2057	2064	2071	2078

It is interesting to note the 70 weeks of Daniel's prophecy was a period of ten Jubilees though it appears to have ended on a Sabbath year after the Jubilee.

What is the practical significance to us in these days of the meaning of the Sabbath year and the Jubilee? There is a modern use of the word "sabbatical", which implies a rest from normal work every seventh year.

I believe a period of unemployment is a forced sabbatical It does not seem to correspond to an actual Sabbath/ civil year, but scripture makes it clear God makes up for things, in His own time, in His own way, which have not been observed.

What is the spiritual significance to us in these days of the meaning of the Sabbath year and the civil/ Jubilee? The millennium in heaven is a rest to the earth which makes up for all the Sabbath/sacred years, which have not been observed, as well as continuing God's patterns.

The end of time and the subsequent end of sin are certainly types of the release from debt and servitude commanded by the Sabbath/sacred year. The Jubilee/civil is a type of the return of our earthly home to us after having been sold to sin and the devil.

I wonder what other significance God will reveal to those who study this subject deeply.

I wonder what other significance this may have to us in the end of time.

As always in everything thing that I write it is by the Holy Spirit through me and always for the Glory of Our Father.

MARK OF THE BEAST:

And he causes all, the small and the great, and the rich and the poor, and the freemen and the slaves, to be given a mark on their right hand or on their forehead, and he provides that no one will be able to buy or to sell, except the one who has the mark, either the name of the beast or the number of his name. Here is wisdom. Let him who has understanding calculate the number of the beast, for the number is that of a man; and his number is six hundred and sixty-six.
Revelation 13:16

(Men are on the image of money worldwide in all numerical denominations.
666 = DCLXVI

M(DC)C(LX)X(VI)
MCX=1110 (Arabic/ Roman)
DCLXVI=666

1110 + 666= 1776
1776 to 1876= a time (100 yrs.)
1776 to 1976= times (200 yrs.)
1976 to 2026= half a time (50 yrs.)

(1776 to 2026 is 250 years)

2026 Abomination of Desolation is set up. Prophecy of Daniel fulfilled
Read Daniel chapter 11
(Conflicts to come)
and let the Holy Spirit Guide you.

(No one can buy sell or trade without money in their hand or thinking about how to get money
(on their forehead) (mind)

(Mind on the money and money on the mind)
Money makes those who seek it enslaved to it and they will do anything for it.

"No one can serve two masters; for either he will hate the one and love the other, or he will be devoted to one and despise the other. You cannot serve God and (wealth).
Matthew 6:24 NASB

He who loves money will not be satisfied with money, nor he who loves abundance with its income. This too is vanity.
Ecclesiastes 5:10 NASB

For the love of money is a root of all sorts of evil, and some by longing for it have wandered away from the faith and pierced themselves with many griefs.
1 Timothy 6:10 NASB

MARK OF THE BEAST
(MONEY)
no one can buy sell or trade without it.

IN THE UNITED STATES
(US DOLLAR)
$1 Washington
$5 Lincoln
$10 Hamilton
$20 Jackson
$50 Grant
$100 Franklin
(6 men)
(6 denominations)
(6 in numerical value)
Add the first digit of each denomination
1+5+1+2+5+1= 15 (1+5) = (6)

(666) the number is that of a man.
Calculate the number of the beast

6th day God created man.
Then God said, "Let Us make man in Our image, according to Our likeness; and let them rule over the fish of the sea and over the birds of the sky and over the cattle and over all the earth, and over every creeping thing that creeps on the earth." God created man in His own image, in the image of God He created him; male and female He created them. God blessed them; and God said to them, "Be fruitful and multiply, and fill the earth, and subdue it; and rule over the fish of the sea and over the birds of the sky and over every living thing that moves on the earth." God saw all that He had made, and behold, it was very good. And there was evening and there was morning, the sixth day.
Genesis 1:26

Just to point out that the no. 666 is actually DCLXVI in roman numerals, and that D, C, L, X, V, and I, in turn, are the first six symbols in the roman numerical system in reverse order.

John (apparently) authored the book of Revelation in Greek, but he quite likely used the Roman system for numbers although the Greeks did have their own numeral system for a while, they were under Roman rule at John's time (Arabic/Indian numerals were not in use in that region until centuries later).

It is not the number itself that is significant, but the fact that it can be represented by numbers. And what can be represented by numbers? Wealth of course, in the form of money!
'No one might be able to buy or sell unless they had the mark of the beast (...non-monetary wealth...) or the number corresponding to his name (...monetary wealth...)'. (Revelation 13:17)

CPSIA information can be obtained
at www.ICGtesting.com
Printed in the USA
LVHW072327080222
710599LV00020B/709